CREATING TOP FLIGHT TEAMS

Hilarie Owen

KOGAN PAGE

YOURS TO HAVE AND TO HOLD
BUT NOT TO COPY

First published in 1996

Paperback edition published in 1997

Kogan Page Limited
120 Pentonville Road
London N1 9JN

© Hilarie Owen, 1996

British Library Cataloguing in Publication Data
A CIP record for this book is available from the British Library.

ISBN 0-749-41829-X

Typeset by Saxon Graphics Limited, Derby
Printed in England by Clays Ltd, St Ives plc

Contents

Preface

Many books have been written on teams, but this one is different. I had the unique opportunity of studying and working with a world class team for a short while. It was an experience which needs to be recorded, for out of the time I spent with them, a new theory on teams developed. This book records both how the theory developed and the experience of stepping into a different world to study the Royal Air Force Aerobatic Team, the RAF Red Arrows. I feel proud to have been allowed to work with them so closely.

I hope that you enjoy this book as much as I enjoyed the researching and writing. I also hope that the book and accompanying video will enable you to develop an organisation in which all employees strive for the very best, every working day. Of course, to achieve this, the organisation has to put into place the right structures, culture and management philosophy to encourage individuals to achieve their best. The book will explain how this can be done.

Flying is my passion, so how I have felt working on this project from beginning to end is best summed up by the pioneering woman pilot, Amelia Earhart in a letter she wrote to her husband before her last flight: 'Please know that I am aware of the hazards. I want to do it because I want to do it. Women must try and do things as men have tried. When they fail, their failure must be a challenge to others.'

I dedicate this work to my son, Darren and my two nieces Rebecca and Rosemary. I hope some of their challenges in life will be as exciting as this one was for me.

All of this would not have been possible without support from the following people. My biggest thanks go to the RAF for opening doors and in particular the Red Arrows; Squadron Leader Les Garside-Beattie, the Team Manager, the

Chief Technicians and Engineers, Wing Commander RAFAT, Air Commodores Gordon McRobbie and Simon Bostock Commandant CFS, and their team, Warrant Officer John Howard and the office staff, and Air Vice-Marshal Chris Coville. Without their openness, honesty, friendship and access, this project would never have succeeded. I also thank them for opening a new world to me, one that I feel honoured to have been a part of for a short while. My thanks also go to my publishers and in particular Philip Mudd whose enthusiasm encouraged me to complete this.

My special thanks go to Squadron Leader Adrian Thurley, Flight Lieutenant Sean Chiddention, Flt Lt Benny Ball, Flt Lt Jerry Bird, Flt Lt Barry Cross, Flt Lt Simon Mead, Fl Lt Rob Last, Sq Ld Gordon Howes and Flt Lt Neil Rogers of the '93 team; Sq Ld John Rands, Flt Lt Spike Zanker, Flt Lt Mark Jepson and Flt Lt Kelvin Truss from the '94 team.

Finally, I hope that you are inspired by reading this and will set about the challenge of creating top flight teams in your own organisations.

Introduction

"The only limits are, as always, those of vision."
James Broughton

HOW IT ALL BEGAN

I first saw the Red Arrows at Farnborough in 1988. It was my first airshow and I spent most of the day looking up into the skies, nearly bumping into people. The magnificent machines, shining in the sun, were roaring fire and making the most earshattering noise. The Harrier display was like watching ballet in the sky as this machine manoeuvred overhead. Then came the turn of the Red Arrows who suddenly appeared, and gave an exciting and breathtaking show. I had also watched the majestic, beautiful Concorde and a Russian MiG which was visiting a British Airshow for the first time. It was all magnificent.

Like thousands of others, I captured the day on camera. I had no idea then that I was to get so close to this world. Even more remarkable, I would find out that the Harrier display pilot that day was the first Red Arrow I would meet and that one of the syncro-pair in the Red Arrows at Farnborough in 1988 was to be the Team Leader when I worked with them.

The fascination for aeroplanes grew and in 1992 I began to have flying lessons. Then, on a cold November morning, I turned up for a local Business Breakfast at the Queens Hotel in Cheltenham. As soon as I'd heard that the speaker was from the Red Arrows I had booked a place. On arrival I even managed to talk my way on to the top table and sit with the guest speaker – Squadron Leader Les Garside-Beattie or 'Red 10'. I was going to enjoy this talk and leave feeling good.

What happened in the next ten minutes changed my life completely. At first, the presentation seemed like any other, with slides explaining the work of the Red Arrows. During the talk, Squadron Leader Les Garside-Beattie used a metaphor to put across what it was like to fly with the team. He explained: 'Imagine driving down the outside lane of the motorway with 8 other cars, all doing 200 miles an hour, bumper to bumper, knowing that no one would do anything silly, each relying on the other to do their job.'

This picture stayed in my mind for a few moments, then suddenly a thought flashed through, wiping out the picture and replacing it with a question. Wasn't this picture some-thing similar to what I was trying to get organisations to develop in my consultancy work? One of the biggest prob-lems causing lack of communication, empowerment, team-work and all the things causing ineffectiveness in organisations at *all* levels, was lack of trust. I felt instinctively there was something here – something no one else in the room was aware of.

I listened to the rest of the talk with even keener interest. At the end, my head was reeling with ideas and questions. Was there something here that could be transferred to other organisations to help them? I had to find out.

People were surrounding Red 10 by this time, asking for autographs and pictures. I thrust my business card into his hand and asked him to ring me, telling him I had an idea I wanted to discuss. Later that morning he rang, a week later we met and talked through the idea of producing a training video. After a further meeting with the Wing Commander RAFAT, the project began a month later. It lasted a total of two years.

In the first year I carried out qualitative and quantitative research to establish 'what' this team did and 'how' they did it. This included testing existing theories on teams and decid-ing how the video should be planned. The objective was to produce a video to sell to organisations who wanted to develop teams. We agreed that the proceeds of the video sales would go to the Red Arrows Trust Fund which sends funds to worthy causes such as children's hospitals. This made the project even more worth while.

However, what also emerged was a new theory on teams, built on previous theories, but going beyond them. It became clear that the project needed to extend from the production of a video, to writing a book and also developing this new theory into a programme which could be used to help teams in other organisations. The ideas in this book will be helpful to directors, managers, trainers, professionals such as accountants and solicitors, public servants and National Health Service (NHS), schools and charities personnel – anyone who wishes to improve the performance of people through teams.

Today the outcome of my work with the Red Arrows is helping organisations, particularly at board and management level, where directors and managers are having to deal with a different world from that of the 1980s. Those organisations have included manufacturing companies, a trade union, a firm of accountants. high technology companies, marketing and public relations agencies, and the public sector. All have differing needs, but all are wanting to develop the performance of people.

This work has led to a belief and commitment that those organisations which will continue to succeed will do so by their boards becoming world class teams and grasping this changing world by seeking the opportunities change brings with it. This team ethos can be developed throughout the organisation, enabling *all* people to act and develop their potential, instead of feeling stressed and unworthy. As high performing teams they will lead their organisations to greater achievements and higher success.

We will start at the beginning by putting into context why there is a need for top flight teams throughout organisations today.

PART 1

1

A Different World Today

"The only thing that makes life possible is permanent, intolerable uncertainty; not knowing what comes next."

Ursula K Le Guin

Why are teams so important in organisations today? The answer lies in the changes which have occurred since the 1980s that have affected organisations in their structure, cultures, processes and people. These changes have meant that, to succeed, organisations have to operate more than ever before with teams.

'Change is not what it used to be' wrote Charles Handy in his book, *Age of Unreason*. It is true that the world has been evolving and changing since time began, but what is so different today is both the *pace* and the *effects* of change, which impinge on everyone's life.

During the 1980s and early 1990s companies in the private sector and organisations in the public sector have been changing dramatically, mainly because of external forces. Whether in the private, public or voluntary sector, change has been rapid and not always desired. The causes of these changes have included government policy, economic factors, greater competition, greater expectation

15

for customer services and quality – all of which have put greater demands on management effectiveness.

There have been a number of changes in market conditions that have influenced company policies including:

- increased competition, either actual or anticipated, which has clearly been important in driving organisations to seek ways that will improve productivity, quality and efficiency – the single European market is just one element of this;

- changes in the economy as a whole, especially recession, have put companies under pressure – fighting to get, or to retain, their market share of diminishing demand.

In the public sector, rationalisation has led to cutting staff and resources from government departments. Local authorities have had to cope with compulsory competitive tendering (CCT), the Citizens' Charter and numerous other legislative changes, all in the context of reducing resources. Education and the NHS now have different management structures. Where their political masters have been of the same persuasion as those in government, there has often been an added impetus to adopt policies in line with that government's thinking and philosophy about competition and choice.

At the same time, a long world recession has led to rationalising or downsizing companies generally, often removing a tier of management, and leaving those behind with a greater workload and fear for their future employment. Executives are doing very little to overcome these feelings of insecurity and so to cope people are resorting to self-preservation tactics – not a productive environment for developing effective teamwork.

Yet, struggling with change isn't something the UK is experiencing alone. The western world is transforming and we are all being affected by those transformations. We are still feeling the effects of leaving an economy based on manufacturing industry behind, and moving to a high technological information society and greater service sector. This has meant that different skills are needed which has led to changes on a large scale. Coal-mines and shipyards have closed, leaving not only mass unemployment, but whole populations and sometimes generations, feeling they have no future.

However, from these ashes a phoenix is arising – management buy-outs have begun to run some of these companies. Take a close look at these companies now – how differently they are being managed and run. The old ways won't work. Confrontation has been replaced by co-operation, and teams are working across these companies.

Tower Colliery in South Wales and Leyland Daf in the Midlands show how workers and management working together can change companies into strong competitive organisations. Why has this change come about? Is it because failure means the owners and workers will lose not only their jobs but their savings too? If this is true, why is it that in the UK, we perform our best when our backs are against the wall? Or is the reason that workers are participating in the decisions and problems in these companies, and feel part of the team? Both reasons are true, but the driving force is the commitment of every manager and worker, which stems from a feeling of involvement and pride. These were key factors I observed in studying the Red Arrows and prevalent in organisations working as teams rather than hierarchies.

Inside organisations, there is slow realisation that to survive and be successful into the turn of the century, it is necessary to change the structures, cultures, strategies and behaviour of people to cope with a different business culture and world.

For a long time, business gurus have been saying that staid, difficult to respond hierarchies are out and fast, flexible, flatter networks in. Writers describe this network structure as a constellation of interdependent businesses or specialist units, relying on one another for expertise and knowledge, while having a peer relationship with the centre which ensures a unity of purpose and mission.

Yet the move from hierarchical organisations has been slow. Many use this network description, but few have yet to make it a reality for all who work in the organisation.

Even when restructuring and layers are removed, the hierarchy mentality remains and managers are afraid of letting go their assumed power. This is because they perceive power as a limited resource – in other words, the more one gives away, the less one is left with. Power is unlimited and, through empowering people, it grows not diminishes.

In his book, *Creative Organization Theory*, Gareth Morgan contrasts the network organisation with the traditional hierarchy (see Figure 1). In his model of the network peripheral or home workers are included, as are customers. Vital here is the flow of information in which recent technology has played an important part. This enables strategic direction from the centre and can be an organisation's competitive advantage.

There are implications for executives, managers and personnel in a network organisation. Senior executives need to develop their technology skills to utilise the different information flows. For others, a flatter organisation means the layers of management which had been the route for career progression have disappeared. Therefore, future executives have to find other means for development. This is happening already, where organisations, such as Rover and Rank Xerox, are putting the responsibility for career development on the individual and have set up learning centres, where individuals can spend time using interactive training facilities.

As organisations no longer recruit for life, employees are useful for as long as they have valued competencies. Therefore individuals are trying new ways for development, including projects, periods in different functions of the organisation, secondment to customers and special assignments working closely with directors.

The clearest difference between a hierarchy and a network organisation is that a network is more flexible and can respond quicker, which is vital today. This includes getting new products into the marketplace or implementing new systems and ways of working to capitalise on business opportunities. Finally, although networks look different to hierarchies, the differences are not just structural.

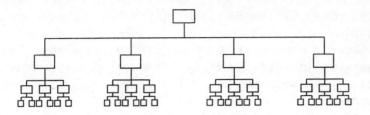

Model 1
This is how the hierarchical organisation looks

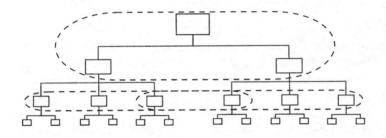

Model 2
Some organisations now have project and task teams but remain hierarchical

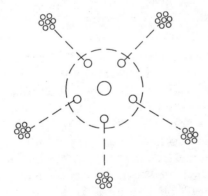

Model 3
A network consists of a centre with loose groups which move around

Figure 1 *From Hierarchy to Network. Adapted from Gareth Morgan*

The cultures, management and leadership, power, even their reasons for existing, are different and right for teams to flourish.

Some organisations have tried to change their culture by saying they 'empower' their employees, but again the reality on the ground does not always match the statements in their annual reports. Some writers on management see much future change coming from the expected increase of women up through the ranks.

In *The Female Advantage – Women's Ways of Leadership*, Sally Helgesen compared her findings with Henry Mintzberg's study of managers and found:

> One of the main gender differences is that women structure organisations as a web, or network, rather than a hierarchy. Each of the women described her place in the organisation as being in the centre reaching out, rather than at the top reaching down. A hierarchy focuses on targeting a position, climbing the ladder and knocking out competition. A web emphasizes interrelationships, building up strength and knitting loose ends into the fabric.

There are many advantages to this approach, but again, people at the top of organisations need to know how to implement this structure and how to develop a culture that encourages the changes. Managers need to adapt their style of management to ensure that the reality happens throughout the organisation.

Yet, to date, although there is some evidence that women bring a different approach to management, there has been a tendency for many to have achieved senior positions by adopting male behaviour. These women sometimes claim that they have found no prejudice in the fact that they are women. So, until a great many more women 'break the glass ceiling' and lead in their own way, we cannot rely on a few women to make the changes necessary to encourage teams.

It is clear that organisations need to look and behave differently now than they did 20 years ago because of all these changes. Rosabeth Moss Kanter in her book, *The Change Masters*, identified organisations who had changed to deal with the external and internal changes. From these she concluded that to succeed the organisation must first put into place the systems, practices, culture and rewards that will encourage people to be enterprising. In other words, they must solve problems, identify and take advantages of opportunities. Secondly, Canter argues that companies must have a structure built around small working teams with autonomy to act. Third, and finally, they must develop a culture that encourages pride, rather than a culture of mediocrity or inferiority.

These three goals should be included here if we are to develop top performing teams and indeed they are very apparent in the success of our model team. With change in organisations, management itself needs to change. This changing role of management is more than words or even action. It is a changing picture and process of how managers should function. Some say this is a paradigm shift. It is certainly a different way of viewing the organisational world, but it is not totally new for some. According to Bob Garratt in *Creating a Learning Organisation*, this new role of management is a shift from:

Production based ⟶ to customer service based

Structure based ⟶ to process based

Efficiency based ⟶ to effectiveness orientated

Conformist ⟶ to creative and responsive

Bureaucratic ⟶ to a flexible structure

Job orientated ⟶ to people orientated

Data orientated ⟶ to information orientated

So organisations, because of the changes coming from mainly external trends, need to alter not only in structure, but also in their behaviour and their processes. For some, this has come to mean total quality management, for others, team briefing or team meetings. These vary from a group of people being told what is going on, to a group letting out frustration but not really resolving the problems. Some have achieved this better than others. There is still a great deal of hit and miss.

THE ORGANISATION TODAY

What should the organisation look like to survive, prosper and be strong for the future? Below is an outline of a new organisation.

The theme throughout is teamwork – a word often used but not always fully understood and practised properly. I believe the key to the organisation for the future is how it runs and focuses as a team. This isn't totally new, as Japanese companies show. But this team process is different from the Japanese model and better suited to the needs of western organisations.

The **COMPONENTS** are:
- Clear corporate goals
- Open communication
- Teamwork
- Involvement
- Commitment
- Flexibility

The **STRUCTURE** is:
- Executive team at centre
- Temporary task teams and
- project groups
- Interlocking groups

Where **MANAGEMENT EMPHASIS** is on:
- Innovation and development
- Goal orientation
- Team achievement
- Problem solving
- High performance

CONTROLS are:
- Mutual goal setting
- Learning from mistakes
- High standards
- Task achievements

MANAGEMENT STYLE is:
- Teamwork with individual responsibility and confrontation of difficulties
- Supportive
- Participative
- Low control

MODELS OF TEAMS

The strength of the Japanese style of teamwork lies in the way they link all departments from design to marketing to production, via interdepartmental teams. Not only does this mean that everyone is involved at all times, it also facilitates communication and assures a design everyone is happy with. In western organisations, on the other hand, a fragmented approach, and functional isolation, promotes poor intergroup communication, and allows the various departments to formulate goals that ultimately conflict.

In addition, in western organisations, when a customer complained after receiving a faulty component, a salesperson or engineer would speak to or visit that customer to try and correct the problem. This could lead to the manufacturing process being changed to avoid further errors, but it is also likely that instead of changing the process, more inspectors would be employed or staff would be trained to mend the errors when they were found. If it is decided to change the manufacturing process the discussions and decisions would be made at management level.

In Japan, however, it would be the *employee* and his or her superviser who would visit the customer and, with the production engineer, would carry out a problem-solving exercise to ensure that the fault did not occur again. The employee would be the key player in this and would afterwards work with the engineer to improve the manufacturing process so that the fault was eradicated. So, there would be no need for more inspectors or staff spending time correcting the faults. Instead, in this situation they have used the employee's knowledge, expertise and ideas to prevent problems arising.

Yet the Japanese system is not without its problems. Japanese companies have very rigid processes with which everyone must comply, right down to putting a product together. This is, at its least, inflexible. That is why the Japanese need to work towards the long-term future and are unable to be flexible towards short-term opportunities. We need to combine their strengths with the flexibility needed for the future. In fact, we need our own model.

The model we are going to examine here is based on one of the best teams in the world. It is through examining the lessons learned from this British team that I believe the picture of organisations for the future can be achieved and succeed in this fast-changing world.

The model team is the RAF Aerobatic team, the Red Arrows. At first you may wonder what they could possibly teach different organisations. It is their *approach* to teamwork and *process* that is detailed here. From this it is possible to draw out the key messages to be learnt and adopted when working in a high performing team. So, if you unblock your hearts and minds to any preconceptions and open your thoughts, you will see a fresh, exciting approach to teamwork that can be installed at all levels of an organisation.

But it is not enough just to 'train' managers in these skills. This approach must be both adopted and driven by the top, and grasped and adopted at the bottom too. By doing this you will use all the talent and brain power of the organisation to enable it to succeed – this is true empowerment, and much more than a buzz word in management circles. As Charles Handy wrote: 'Competitive advantage enables organisations and nations to prosper, and it comes by brain power adding value to raw material to produce services or products that will sell.'

Yet organisations are not always using their available

brain power. Many people at work feel underutilised or use their greater potential in other outlets, away from the workplace, on committees or in pressure groups. Tom Peters summed up the situation: 'Most employees are creative, committed and achieving – except for the eight hours when they work for you.'

This brain power is not just lost from high flyers in organisations; it is also lost from the shop floor, from offices, from retail stores and in homes. The RAF Red Arrows really are ordinary men doing an extraordinary job. Any good pilot in the RAF can become a team member and over the years many have succeeded. Some become a team member at the second attempt, after failing the first time. This is because the feedback they receive enables them to develop the necessary skills to grow, adapt and achieve as valued workers. If we are to believe present thinkers such as Charles Handy, Peter Drucker, Rosabeth Moss Kanter and Tom Peters, we are entering the age of the 'knowledge workers', with lean and flexible organisations, coping with chaos and change, rethinking the nature of employment and reframing our ideas on the value of people in these organisations.

The most natural way to release this brain power is to create teams which work together, with the shared idea that, by doing the best for the team, one is also doing the best for oneself. The aim is to create synergy, whereby the team's output is greater than the individual's contribution alone. By doing this, performance is enhanced and the results is organisations are as dynamic and awesome as watching the Red Arrows doing their flying displays. The rest of this book shows you how to achieve this objective.

2

Developing Teams in Organisations

"If we did all the things we are capable of doing, we would literally astound ourselves."

Edison

What is a team? There are many definitions of a team, most including in their definitions the phrases 'a common aim' and 'working together'. When you ask a team member to give a definition of the team many will be descriptive and subjective, using feelings rather than actions. Yet there are four distinct characteristics of teams.

1. The first characteristic of the team is that it should be more than just a group of individuals working together. There are plenty of work groups in organisations, but they are not necessarily a team. Teams are not about structure or even size. A committee is not a team, nor is a group of individuals who happen to work together. A committee exists to find a workable compromise and achieve what it can. A group of individuals working together happen to be pushed together and could survive with little communication.

Today, many so-called teams in organisations are brought about through more project and task work. These are highly skilled people, yet putting them together does not necessarily result in teams. At the same time, there has been a push for 'self-managed' or 'self-directed' teams, crossing functional boundaries to work together. Some are enormously successful, while others drift and fall apart. Teams are not about the technical expertise of the members. You could say that the Red Arrows are skilled pilots, but this is not enough.

Teamwork has a synergistic effect in that the individuals working together achieve more than they could alone. When Rebecca Stevens, the first female British climber to reach the summit of Everest, and her party conquered Everest in the late spring of 1993, the team, including Rebecca, were successful because of each individual's contribution. Yet many teams today are not aware of their members' skills, strengths or individuality. Every team is unique and, when team members change, the team will also change and the team leader should not suppress this. The Red Arrows team changes every year, but their performance remains high.

2. The second characteristic of a team is that it shares a common purpose which is clear to each team member. Each member recognises that to achieve the stated goal the effort of everyone is required. It's amazing how many so-called teams in organisations do not know the common goal. You can try this out by simply asking the team members what they think their goal is and listen to their answers. Teams are there to achieve a goal, to win, by using everyone's talents.

3. Teamwork, however, does not 'just' happen and the third characteristic of a team is that it requires continuous hard work. But it should also be enjoyable, fun and should result in a feeling of personal satisfaction for every team member. Much of this work is down to the team leader. The main aim is to make the team objective

more important and exciting than personal interests or the interests of those they represent.

4. The fourth and final characteristic of a team is that it has a 'feel' about it, a sort of 'teamness'. Members are open and direct with each other, without anyone feeling personally attacked. In fact mistakes are openly discussed and seen as opportunities to learn and develop. There is a pride, a sense of belonging to the team, which members find motivating. Conversation is about the team inside and outside the workplace. All this leads to work being a happy and fulfilling place to be.

But before a team can develop, the organisation it will have to operate within must create the right climate in which it can exist and thrive. No matter how good the intentions of the team are, it is not isolated and has to interact with others in the organisation. This is a problem for both teams and organisations, and that is why developing teams needs to be looked into. But developing teams also have to include developing organisations which have to work to create the right climate for teams to thrive.

CREATING A CLIMATE FOR TEAMS

There are many good examples of effective teams outside the workplace, particularly in sport, but why is this not carried through to the workplace? The main reason is that those running and managing the organisations are not encouraging teamwork. In some cases, they actively discourage teamwork, as it is perceived as a threat to their power.

In a sense we are dealing with what McGregor unsurfaced many years ago when he wrote: 'All managerial decisions and actions rest on assumptions about behaviour.' His research showed that how we perceive people affects how we treat them, and he then produced his Theory X and Theory Y ideas. McGregor isolated the Theory X manager as perceiving work as distasteful to most people; that people were unambitious and didn't want responsibility, they lacked creativity in solving problems and preferred to be directed. This results in managers behaving in a certain way, including discouraging teams.

The Theory Y manager, however, perceives work as natural if the conditions are right and recognises that self-control is important in achieving goals. The Y manager also regards people as having the capacity to take responsibility, motivate themselves and creatively solve problems. This looks more like the Japanese model of management and, therefore, is more likely to result in teamwork.

There are still too many Theory X managers in organisations today, and their behaviour will not change until their attitudes and perceptions change. If people are not given the chance to contribute, you cannot have a team. So we have to look at how to bring about this change of attitude and behaviour, before we look at how to develop teams. For, without this change, teams cannot develop and grow.

I remember having a man on one of my courses who considered himself to be a brilliant manager and team leader. When he had the opportunity to demonstrate this in a team problem-solving exercise, he totally took over and made the decisions for the rest of the team. This was how he managed back at work. He spoke, and they listened. It was not easy to get him to stop his leading and directing role in order to listen to others and give their ideas a chance.

The first thing was to make him aware of what he was doing. The second stage was even more difficult; he had to stop defending his behaviour and admit that he was wrong. This is not easy for anyone. Once this stage was complete, it was simple to build his skills to behave differently and build confidence in himself to realise that he didn't have to control all the time to succeed. So, for teams to work, there needs to be a fundamental change in management style. If this is not achieved, people attending team meetings will find no real change and think 'Why bother, no one listens to my ideas'. The result is a meeting with little, if any, contribution.

Some managers are frightened to change their style because they think it means losing or giving away power and control to others. It doesn't. Many people perceive power as a limited resource and, by giving any away, they have less. They also see it as control over others. To exercise this power, they use a mixture of coercive methods, which over time have to become more and more coercive.

Yet power itself is a resource which can be used in different ways. For example, some will use information as their power resource, while others will use their personality. However, power itself has another perception – that which makes an individual effective. Here, power is taken from its French origin, 'pouvoir', which means to be able. From this comes the true meaning of 'empowerment' – to enable people to act and perform effectively. By giving this power, a person does not have less; in fact, they will discover they have more because people will follow and respect them.

Included in this desired change in management style is the need to look for opportunities to praise. Too often managers criticise when something goes wrong, but forget to praise when it works. This should not be a patronising remark, so it needs to relate to genuine effort. Neither should recognising individual contributions be a once-a-year appraisal job. It is being aware when a team member has achieved something good and telling them. At the same time, people have to get used to this, particularly if the culture has meant managers only criticised previously. At first, individuals may feel embarrassed or suspicious of a compliment or reward. But, in time, they will also respond positively to praise – and return it. Think how you feel when someone says to you: 'Well done, you did a good piece of work there'. Don't you mentally grow 6 inches and feel good inside because your contribution has been noticed? It means that the team members will put in more effort and are more likely to follow you.

Another necessary change to management style is to listen and communicate more. Managers are usually so busy, they don't always make time to inform the team about what is going on or listen to feedback. This leaves team members feeling left out, and involvement is a key component to teamwork. If a captain of a hockey team did all the running with the ball and made all the decisions, the other team members would give up trying to perform – so it is in organisations. In the case of the Red Arrows my work studied two very different Team Leaders. The first was very strong and confident; the second quiet and confident. There is no ideal type of leader. You can be enthusiastic, practical, a good communicator or have specialist knowledge. What matters is how you lead and your behaviour. Both developed trust, loyalty and respect by their consistent behaviour, enabling the team to create synergy.

Structures in organisations can work against teams in that teams should not only be based on functions or departments. That produces straight line solutions. This is where the Japanese model does so well in that organisations need to develop good horizontal principles with joint problem solving and team spirit perceived by all. In high performing teams hierarchies are not needed; leadership is based on respect, not on position in the organisation, as we shall see in the case of the RAF Red Arrows.

Reinforcing the organisational structures are career structures which tend to be functional. We end up with 'specialists' who have difficulty understanding and relating to other functional managers. These 'experts' are promoted to senior positions in the organisation because of their expertise and not their management potential. Teams need a broad outlook and range of skills, as do team leaders and managers. New ideas on structures such as multifunctional taskforces and cell manufacturing do not always equate with teamwork if the individuals within those teams are not motivated, valued, have a clear direction and power to act, and are responsible for their actions. This can be seen in companies ranging from manufacturing to marketing. These task teams and cells have been structurally put together as teams, but that is all – and the directors ask why they are not succeeding!

Team training

Many organisations have tried developing teams by training. Organisations spend a great deal of money sending people on courses or running programmes internally. Yet most people return to work and very little changes.

There are many reasons for this. The course may not have been appropriate; delegates may have failed to see the relevance; on returning to work, the senior manager may not appear interested in following up the course, which is very demotivating for the individual and usually leads to that person thinking 'Why should I change or improve the way I do things if those senior to me aren't interested in what I do or how I feel?'. Very often the culture of the organisation doesn't allow teams to develop because it still maintains the hierarchy, using information as a form of power over people.

All this means that while training courses may be enjoyable, they do not always lead to an improvement for the organisation. In addition, people carry on working in a semi-isolated way; either plodding on and making sure nothing rocks the boat too much; or totally self-orientated, doing what will bring personal recognition and hopefully promotion.

What effects does this have on the organisation? Take the plodder, going through his or her work, relying on others to get information to them or pass it on. If there is a hold up, the plodder gets on with something else or waits for the information to reach them. Nothing changes, in fact change is perceived as frightening as it upsets the status quo, and efficiency is reliant on the pace of this person's work.

Such people have lost all inspiration and motivation because their own needs and aspirations have not been developed. They may grumble from time to time and any mistakes they make will result in punishment, usually from an equally frustrated and demotivated superior.

On the other hand, the self-orientated person is beavering away, prioritising what is highly visible, totally uninterested in helping colleagues – unless there is a pay-off for themselves. Change will also be resisted vociferously unless there are perceived pay-offs for the individual. Backbiting and 'politics' become pastimes, as does 'beating' the other departments. Neither of these situations are healthy for the organisation as a whole, for teams or the people who work in them.

'Them and us'

Another barrier to team development is the presence of 'them and us' in organisations between managers and those they manage. This two-tier system is propelled by those on both sides who benefit from the conflict. Often the relationship is so poor that teamwork is impossible. There is total lack of trust, and suspicion leads to everyone trying to interpret meanings to conversations and actions. Honesty is replaced by 'watching your backs' and fear rules. Yet it is possible to change this with the right actions and commitment.

Leading by example

Finally, boards of directors cannot expect these changes to happen below them without changing themselves. They must lead by example. At board level, the effects of poor teamwork can be felt throughout the organisation. During my career as a consultant I was asked to work with a company involved in direct mail and marketing. This company had a board made up of a small team. One member of this team was a strong, self-orientated person, who arrogantly trampled on people and used bullying tactics. This behaviour seemed to be accepted by the rest of the top team.

The next layer down from the board were considered poor at management, particularly at managing people. They were sent on a course and it was suggested that, as well as developing their personal management skills, they should work more as a team. Much of the problem arose from functional isolation and poor communication. This meant that those in the creative department were not 'working' with those looking after the accounts or clients. A team approach should have improved matters.

Yet what transpired was that they were so used to a strong leader at board level that they could not even agree on an agenda and procedures for the team meetings. They felt powerless and trapped. Lack of any praise from the board was carried down by the managers themselves, who were also not motivating or praising their people. Below them, people on the ground felt trodden on without support from their managers. Communication problems were leading to frustration and anger.

Not surprisingly, many left the company during the next 12 months. Eventually, the person who had set up the company saw and accepted what was happening, and fired the self-orientated director and her associates. The message here is that a team at management level is greatly affected by the top layer, and that leadership and teams need to be established throughout the organisation, not just at one or two levels. In addition, the culture of the organisation must be one which encourages teams, and this must be actively developed by the top layer and work downwards.

The most important team in any organisation is the top team in that it has the greatest effect on the rest of the organisation. Yet there are many reasons why having a 'real' team at this layer is difficult to achieve. For many, getting to the 'top' is an end goal in itself. However, once there, there is a general acceptance that to have achieved this, there is no need for further development. The problem is that many become directors and don't know how their role differs from the one they had before.

So, they quickly revert back to that previous role because they know it, are kept busy and feel comfortable with it, and other managers feel exacerbated because their director won't let go and allow them to do what is required. This also means that the role of director is not properly utilised and board meetings become functional defensive behaviour with the marketing director defending marketing; the production director defending production; and the managing director trying to do too much of everything. Under this climate, trust is absent.

Professor Andrew Kakabadse found other issues for top teams in his research on *Leadership in Times of Change*. More than half his sample of British directors would smile through gritted teeth rather than risk being honest and say what they really wanted to say. The result, he says, is a board that behaves like a dysfunctional family. As an example he speaks about a marketing director whose efforts to improve his own performance are restrained by the defensiveness and political motivation of relationships at board level.

In Mike Johnson's book, *Managing in the Next Millennium*, about 600 managers responded to a survey on leadership. Eighty-nine per cent of these said that business leaders should be able to build effective teams, but only 43 per cent thought their chief executive could.

Developing top teams is challenging – but also most rewarding. My aim is to develop top teams worldwide. Once this is done, I believe many of the issues concerning why teams fail in organisations can be addressed with a positive outcome. Culture change, including management style, has to be driven by and lived out by the top. When employees see the change happening around them, they will believe the messages they are hearing and will be more likely to respond to the changes. Teams will then permeate the organisation – effective, top performing teams.

As markets change and technologies develop, organisations need to become more flexible and responsive to opportunities, while ensuring that in doing so they do not fragment. Directors and managers need to learn to think strategically. There is a greater need for teams in the evolution of organisations, and managers will need to become skilled in leading teams by gaining agreement and commitment, communicating a vision and directing rather than telling. Gone are the days of managers managing and workers doing. Performance, commitment, pride and trust are needed in organisations today. There is no greater example of this than the RAF Red Arrows.

3

Year One with the Reds

"If I have seen further, it is by standing on the shoulders of giants."

Sir Isaac Newton

BACKGROUND

The Red Arrows were formed in 1965 with seven pilots equipped with the Folland Gnat Jet trainer. The team expanded to nine pilots in 1968, and since then the Diamond Nine formation has become their trademark and is recognised throughout the world. In 1980, the Gnat was replaced with the Hawk which is a front-line jet used by the RAF.

Each year, three new pilots are selected to join the Red Arrows. These pilots stay with the team for three years. Since 1983 the squadron has been based in Lincolnshire where the engineers and all supporting personnel and equipment are together. During the summer months, the Red Arrows perform their aerobatic display over 100 times both in the UK and abroad. For the RAF, the Red Arrows demonstrate the peak of precision flying, as well as delighting crowds all over the world which encourages recruitment.

My work with the Red Arrows began with trips to RAF Scampton to learn more about how the team work together. During the year I spent time shadowing the team and conducted individual interviews. The year begins in October/November, when three of the nine pilots begin their first year with the team. Together with the Team Leader they begin the process of developing new flying skills and building confidence in themselves. They start this learning process at a relatively high altitude of 1500 feet or more above the ground. At this altitude their previous flying skills can be safely adapted to meet the new demands that they will have to master in the new roles: safety at all times is the ultimate priority.

Primarily this early training involves close formation flying which quickly expands the skills of the new team members. Once they have achieved the necessary standard then slowly and progressively the experienced team members are added to the formation; it is the Team Leader who decides when the formation size can be increased.

The process begins with annual applications from which a short list is constructed by senior officers, but these new pilots were chosen by the team rather than senior officers in the hierarchy. This had followed a week where nine hopefuls spent days with the team, passing a flying test, being interviewed and getting to know each other. Only those who pass the flying test can be considered for becoming a Red Arrow. Socialising is also important and the team have to feel they can work with the new guys; during the summer months they probably see more of each other than they do of their families. Therefore, the best pilot doesn't necessarily get chosen.

SELECTION

I was invited to attend the day of the interview. Three people were involved – the Team Leader, Wing Commander

RAFAT and Air Commandant CFS. As each pilot entered the room effort was made to relax the candidate as they were very nervous. Then a series of questions were asked, for example:

- What part of the job is the most difficult?
- Which part would you like the most?
- Why do you want to join the team?
- Who would you select from the other candidates?
- What could you bring to the job?

It was interesting to note that the selection team of Officers were looking for the right personality as much as flying skills, and were using gut feeling as well as analysis about the candidates in their decision-making process. The successful candidates were those who were totally honest rather than giving answers they thought the panel wanted to hear.

We all came up with the same three names, with one in reserve, but the final decision is always with the team of Red Arrows pilots. This year, they decided on the same three as the panel, but it doesn't always happen that way.

Relating this process to your organisation, who recruits your team members? Is it a manager or someone from personnel? If many applicants apply, managers can whittle down the numbers, but the final choice should be made by the team together, because when that person eventually joins, much of the barriers over fear of acceptance will not be there. This enables the team to work effectively more quickly and it's a boost to the individual to know that they were chosen by the team.

To ensure the right person joins, those on the short-list can be invited to spend a day or more with the team and get involved in some of the work. This can be followed with an evening together and social interaction. By the end of this time, the team will have a good idea of who would add value to the team and integrate well with them.

DOING THE JOB

This combination of technical flying skills and social inter-action is crucial to the Reds. Every day during the winter months the team balance flying training and seeing visitors. When the weather permits, the team fly three sorties a day, experimenting, trying out new moves, learning new skills and putting together the new display for the summer season ahead. During their three years the team will meet hundreds of people from all walks of life, including the media, company directors who sponsor them, children in hospital where they present cheques from their trust fund, and famous stars and politicians. But, for all, their business is flying.

Before each flight, the team attend a briefing. Here, the Boss, the nickname for the Team Leader, outlines the weather conditions from the Met Office and the manoeuvres they will practise. Quietly, they go to their machines and take off. The sortie is always filmed and visitors go outside to watch.

On their return, there is a buzz of conversation with pilots describing what happened. They eventually sit down and go through a debriefing. This is in two parts. The first is led by the Leader as each stage of the sortie is examined. Pilots criticise each other and themselves. To an outsider, this may at first appear rather direct, but it is crucial to the learning process. If a pilot criticises another, the Leader asks if they all agree – they usually do. The Leader may say 'Was that a little wide?', the pilots agree and he goes on to point out important learning points, but breaks to again ask, 'What do you think?' He then agrees with them as to what will be done next. Rank doesn't matter in the debrief; the Leader is criticised too. This openness enables the team to assess how they're progressing.

The second stage is when they all sit and watch the video of the last sortie, again criticising themselves and each other to identify learning points. Every team member has an input into this, but the new pilots are the quietest. These 'new guys' have usually just left a command where they were the Team Leader, leading front-line missions. Now their flying is being criticised every time they go up and they have to take this in their stride. There are no prima donnas in the Red Arrows; what you have are ordinary young men with a job to do.

I asked how the new pilots were getting on. 'The size of the team helps you get to know each other, and there are dinner parties and social events to help.' 'What about the flying?', I ask. 'The building block approach of flying with the Team Leader first has worked. Mistakes can be put right during the next sortie while they are still fresh in your mind.' This young pilot was also aware of his personal development in a new job. 'This is so different, I've had to adjust. There's much more public relations, seeing visitors, giving lectures and becoming more confident.'

Another remarked: 'You have to get up to speed on the bantering! The boss made us feel very welcome so it felt like a team from the first week. Then I found myself being apprehensive during the second week, but Friday evening around the bar helped.' He also found that he was developing both technically to deal with a new way of flying which formation aerobatics requires and personally. 'I am better at talking to the public, and better at debriefing and realising my errors which leads to confidence.'

This reviewing and feedback clearly enables team members to grow and develop, and improve their performance. It hasn't been easy for new team members but their confidence and self-esteem is also growing. One of the regular complaints I hear from people at all levels in organisations is that they lack feedback. The Reds are an example of how regular feedback enhances performance and confidence. It needs to be part of the team process.

How different is it for a second year pilot? "The first year is spent coming to grips with the job and overcoming doubt in your abilities. You keep asking yourself, "am I going to be able to do it?" You are criticised heavily and you have to learn to accept that criticism and accept being a "new boy" again. During the second year, you know you can do the job, so you're more relaxed. Now you have to remember what it was like as a new boy and not be too hard on the new pilots. If something goes wrong, we talk about it afterwards. In the second year you have also learned from your mistakes and needn't be afraid of these mistakes. The key is to put them behind you and not repeat them.'

Flying isn't all the team members do. They each have secondary duties to complete on the ground which they do for the team, so there is no duplicating effort. This comes down to trust in each other and no one has to check to see if it has been done. This is very different from working with someone watching over your shoulder the whole time. In this latter environment, if something goes wrong, there is a tendency to cover it up or face a back-lash. No one is going to do their best in this environment. There will never be trust in the latter and teams need to have trust to thrive. Trust leads to motivation and learning. 'We always strive for perfection. We never do it, but we try' said one of the Reds. How does this relate to your organisation?

Within the team are two 'synchro' pilots. These break off from the main group during the display and do some spectacular flying. Each year towards the end of the first season a pilot is chosen from the new members to fly synchro in his second year. This means that his second year is like the first in that he has to learn more technical flying skills. The two go and practise on their own, and join the rest of the team later. The second synchro pilot is in his third year with the team and his role becomes one of teacher. 'This is daunting in some respect because synchro flying can't be learned from a book. You have to teach it by mouth. Confidence is also important. I have to be a stable platform and the other pilot has to trust me. The errors here can only be small ones.' For these pilots, communication, trust and accepting criticism is as important as being a good pilot.

'I've also become a better team player, learning when to give and take. We know we'll never be perfect. About 2 out of 200 times in the air do we all come down saying – yes, that was perfect! But we never stop striving for this.'

What did the team say about their Team Leader?

'I have no qualms about following him. He's cool, calm, professional and not gung-ho. He accepts criticism too.'

'He lets you get on with the job. He looks at us, but not obviously, not looking over your shoulder all the time. He knows that if we don't do the job, we'll not perform well.'

'He brings you on, if you are over-led, you become an underling.'

'Rank doesn't matter, he accepts criticism and suggestions.'

The Team Leader tells me he had a good role model: 'If I can match him, I'll do OK.' How does Red 1 lead? 'I give a broad outline of what is to be achieved and by when. They get on and let me know if there are any snags.' He made some changes in his three years which included a regular meeting with the Manager and Chief Engineer. This was to cut down on phone calls every five minutes. He also introduced the flying test for new pilots after having to get rid of a pilot in his first year as Team Leader. 'I asked the rest of the team and 50 per cent thought he should go, so I did it in as nice a way as possible. Every team has a weak link and you are as strong as that weak link.'

He also introduced a procedure where the Team Leader has a few minutes alone before a display. He watched a predecessor fly unprepared and saw the consequences. He spends those few minutes clearing everything in his mind so there will be no surprises.

What became clear from these interviews was that there were several processes which were vital for a team to perform well. These included:

- building and developing trust;

- having regular reviews where members were open to criticism as a positive step to learning;

- recognising a certain standard which all members worked towards;

- team decision making, including team selection of new members.

However, there were many more which needed to be identified and some of these were going to be more difficult to uncover.

The next step in my learning process was to spend a full week with the team away in Cyprus. This would enable the team to learn to trust me and open up even more. What was unexpected was how close I would get to the team and how I would experience a new world – the world of the RAF abroad.

Having arrived at Paphos Airport on Cyprus I received a lift to the airbase. My room was next to two female officers and down the corridor from the men. My first evening in the mess wasn't easy as it all felt very strange and I felt a complete outsider among all these males. Being used to hotels, I had come without towels and, not knowing all the mess rules on dress, I was going to have to be careful with the clothes I had with me. However, by the second day I was totally relaxed and beginning to get to know my way around. After breakfast I watched the first sortie from outside my room. It was like a private display as there was no one else around. This was to become a daily treat and something I missed terribly when back home.

The first morning I observed the brief. After explaining the weather conditions, the Team Leader described what happened the previous flight. He then outlined what the team were going to do on the next sortie and asked for comments. Satisfied that the points were clarified the team took off. The Air Vice Marshal, who was in Cyprus to review the Team's progress, offered me a lift in his car to the control tower where the view was best to watch the display.

On return, the debrief was highly participative. Each part of the display was examined. 'You were low Jerry.' 'Yeah, I know.' 'You were just a fraction out Barry.' He acknowledges with a nod. 'I came out of the roll wrong', says the Team Leader. Team members suggest leaving the smoke off and the boss agrees. The Team Leader concludes: 'That was a good effort.' The Air Vice Marshal follows by giving his views on the whole display. He suggests a change, but the team explain how they have experimented with this and why it works better the way they do it. The Air Vice Marshal finishes with praise.

BELBIN'S TEAM ROLES AND THE RED ARROWS

During a break from flying I explained Belbin's work on team roles to the team and asked them to complete Belbin's questionnaire. I wanted to see if this theory had any validity here. Readers may suggest at this point that the reason this team works so well is that the team members are very similar because they work in the same environment and receive the same training. However, the RAF is not a sausage factory. The results were very interesting and deserve closer examination.

More than a group of individuals

To achieve their goals, individuals in teams have to recognise their differences. Just as a football team would not be made up of strikers or goalkeepers, a team should be a collection of differences. A successful team needs to contain individuals with different personalities, skills and priorities, performing different roles.

One of the most recognised studies of team roles was carried out by Meredith Belbin, a British researcher. He studied hundreds of managers working to solve exercises in teams. Early on, it was considered that by putting all the brightest experts together, you would have the most successful team. In fact these teams, often called Apollo teams, did not produce consistently good results. Yet many organisations still believe the brightest people will automatically outperform any others. This is not always the case.

Belbin found that the less brilliant team performed in a mediocre way, until they were joined by a creative or task-orientated person. From this, he realised that a successful team needed different 'roles' which related to different processes, and that these could be related to psychometric tests that could be given to individuals. By identifying these roles, a healthy mix could be put together and the team would be more effective (see Figure 2).

For example, there was a need for someone concerned with the general strategy, who was stable and controlled. There would also be a need for someone to understand and see to the detail of completion, and this person tended to be anxious and introvert. Originally, Belbin ended up with eight roles. He has since added another, making nine. However, not every team needs all in the same degree and the task will influence this. You will also find that if you do have all eight you do not necessarily have a 'super team'. For this reason Belbin's work has been criticised, but what cannot be disputed is that, whatever the task, a team should reflect the roles, and each one should be recognised and utilised. Belbin states that too many of one type can lead to conflict and unproductive effort. How does this theory fit with the Red Arrows?

BELBIN'S TEAM PROFILE RESULTS ON THE RED ARROWS

To test this model, the teams from two years were analysed and compared (see Figures 3 and 4). The first year team were predominantly Company Workers – dutiful, predictable, hard working, self-disciplined but lacking flexibility. However, two other team roles with high scores were Shapers – outgoing, dynamic, challenging inertia and impatient; and Completer/Finisher – orderly, perfectionist and anxious. The role of Team Worker was moderate.

BELBIN TEAM ROLES

The Company Worker is stable and controlled and perceived by other team members as a practical organiser. They turn concepts and plans into practical working procedures systematically. The Company Worker can be thrown easily by sudden changes or too much uncertainty. He or she functions through knowledge and expertise.

The Chairperson controls the way in which a team moves towards the objectives using the team resources. They are intelligent without being intellectual but disciplined and have natural authority. The Chairperson recognises the team's strengths and weaknesses and is good at setting priorities.

The Shaper gets things done, is outgoing but can become anxious. They seek to impose some shape or pattern on group discussions. They have a high control need and can become impulsive, impatient and easily frustrated. Their outward confidence often conceals self doubt.

The Plant brings new ideas and strategies to the team through their bright intellect. These ideas can inspire the team but a plant can sulk if their ideas are not accepted. The plant stays detached as team members get bogged down in problems and can then give a spark to move forward.

The Resource Investigator is popular with team members and wonderful at networking outside the team. They build useful external contacts and resources for the team. They communicate, collect ideas, and adapt to find solutions from an outside view, preventing the team from stagnating.

The Monitor Evaluator analyses problems using their intellect. They can be perceived as cold, but their objectivity can prevent the team from making a mistake. They can be negative to change but their judgement is worth listening to.

The Team Worker cares about the team members as people and fosters team spirit. They are sensitive and loyal but don't like confrontation. The team worker likes harmony and works to develop this in team members.

The Completer Finisher is an anxious introvert who is particular about getting things done properly. They have personal discipline and give tasks more than the usual degree of attention. This can be perceived either as compulsive perfectionism or paying attention to detail. They also have a sense of urgency.

Figure 2 *Belbin Team Roles*

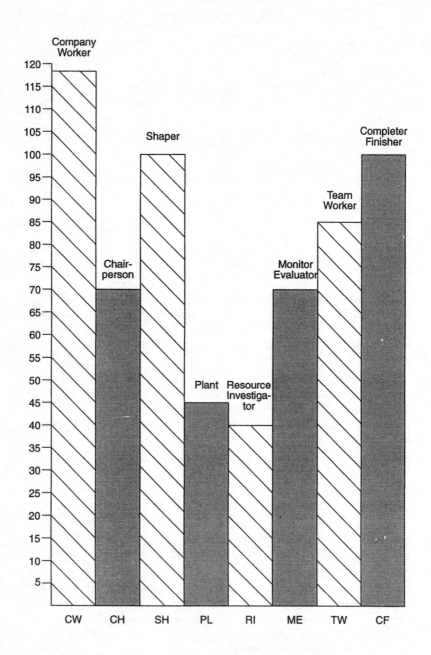

Figure 3 *Team profile of Red Arrows – Year one*

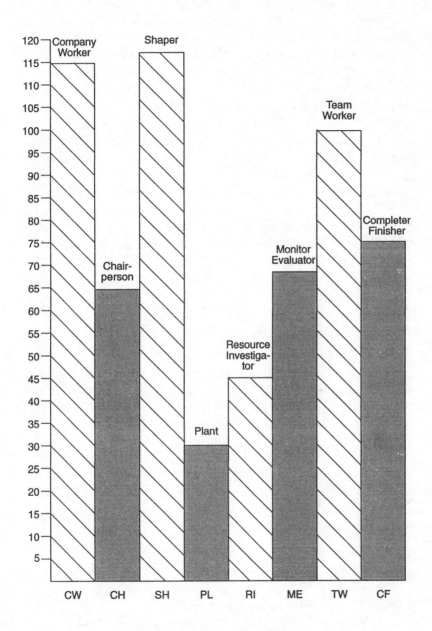

Figure 4 *Team profile of Red Arrows – Year two*

The second year team, when three new pilots joined, changed the profile so that Shaper was the predominant team role, Company Worker was second and Team Worker third. The roles of Completer/Finisher and Plant, which are attention to detail in the former, and intellect and imagination in the latter, dropped considerably as against the previous year. Therefore, a different year meant a different team profile. But did this affect the team results? The outcome was the same – a new display. Belbin's work could explain why certain things happened the way they did, but it still didn't explain the process the team undergo each year. In addition, the team profiles of the two team leaders were almost identical, yet their methodology, style and behaviour were very different. So Belbin's work has its value, but it does not explain the process of maintaining a high performing team, because the team profile can change while performance continues.

WOODCOCK'S BUILDING BLOCKS

What was emerging from the research closely resembled Mike Woodcock's building blocks theory on teams. He states that there are distinct building blocks or characteristics of teams which consist of:

- clear objectives and agreed goals;
- openness and confrontation;
- support and trust;
- co-operation and conflict;
- sound procedures;
- appropriate leadership;
- regular reviews;
- individual development;
- sound inter-group relations.

It was through further interviews with the team members that this theory, although very close, was recognised to be not completely correct. To begin with, there was no need for the building block 'co-operation and conflict', because the team were so open with each other. They were adamant that conflict did not exist, and that if the openness and confrontation worked, there was no need for compromise or conflict.

Neither were these building blocks enough on their own. Within each existed other processes. For example, you may say that it is easy for the Red Arrows to be a team because they have a clear purpose or goal. The research found that this was not as straightforward as might be thought and demonstrates the missing element of the building block theory.

A COMMON PURPOSE OR GOAL

We often believe that a team knows what it is trying to achieve, but as the saying goes 'Never assume'. Yet having a clear objective and agreed goals is more than just knowing what the outcome needs to be. For example, the pilots know that the outcome of their team is to give displays in aerobatic flying to audiences the world over, but the purpose for each of them is more than this. From talks with the individual team members it was clear that their objectives included giving their best performance so as not to let other team members or themselves down. There was a strong element of pride in their work both to themselves and to the team as a whole.

People in organisations are committed to objectives if they feel some identity with and ownership for them. This is achieved by discussions and the team members agreeing to those goals. In the case of the Red Arrows, the objective is clear, but the goals are discussed to establish how each pilot is going to achieve them. These are regularly reviewed and the team objectives become inseparable from each individual's objective. This link of personal and team goals was very strong and vital to achieving the performance required of them. Yet, in organisations, how often are the team's objectives linked to the individual's objectives?

The main reason for this failing is that the team has not recognised the individual needs, only the group needs. These individual needs include fulfilment, recognition and a feeling of achievement. Without these needs being included, individuals feel demotivated and performance slides. This affects both the team as a whole and the team's performance. A successful team allows each individual member to give of their best *and* take from the team those things they need.

As an example, in an organisation where I ran a team development programme, the group realised that team objectives needed to be identified, but they had not considered individual objectives. The background and culture of this team was a trade union representing civil servants. In their London base, individual needs and feelings were covered up.

The members of the regional branch managed to break down this barrier, and they all opened up and disclosed their needs and personal objectives. For the first time the team remarked that they felt as though they were beginning to know each other. They had tried going out to lunch once a month to do this, but it was by being open and honest, and feeling they could express their individual objectives that the team process began.

When both the team needs and the individual needs are recognised, the team objective links to the individual's objectives. It is the role of the Team Leader to see that this happens, but it is also the individual's responsibility. When the Team Leader knows these needs, they can be the key motivator to achieving the team's objective. Therefore, clear objectives and agreed goals are not enough to enhance the performance of a team. The team also needs to identify and encapsulate the individual goals.

I asked the pilots what motivated them to perform well?

'None of us want to be seen doing badly. Here, it's noticed by everyone. But I don't want to do better than the others as it will show weaknesses. So there is a will for each to do their best.'

'The will to succeed. We want to be the best team there has ever been. I am personally determined and, if I get it wrong, I try to find out why and then get it right.'

'Ego and self-respect. Standing among your peers is important and you want the team to do well.'

'Personal standards and not letting the side down. Keeping my own standard high and not failing in my contemporaries' eyes.'

'Pride in doing my best. Everyone knows you can't bullshit, so you do your best all the time.'

'Personal satisfaction. Wanting to play your part and not let anyone else down.'

'Personal pride and to do the job well. There's also the safety factor and the ethos of the team to be perfect.'

'Being a perfectionist and having peer pressure to do well.'

'Primarily myself because, whatever I do, I like to do well. Also I've noticed that if I'm under pressure, being watched or performing a particular landmark, I step up a gear and perform better.'

Here it is clear that individual needs are linked to team needs; and individual performance is linked to team performance. A good Team Leader can use this to motivate and make work a happier place because individual needs are catered for. Yet, in organisations, there is a tendency for performance to be judged by how a person behaves rather than the results they achieve. People are judged by their image, how they dress, their sex appeal, whether their desk is tidy, how they 'appear' to be doing, rather than their actual results.

So, to ensure your team has clear objectives, follow these simple guidelines:

1. motivate everyone to take the objectives on board they must be discussed and agreed by the team;

2. team members need to be involved in determining their own areas of responsibility and own objectives within this;

3. the emphasis should be on results to be achieved, not just things to do;

4. personal objectives should be included in the team goals.

Woodcock's model was still useful but there were other weaknesses which were disturbing. One of these was that there was no mention of the standard of performance. If this team was based on building blocks, there should be one on team standard of performance. This standard was clear to everyone and required hard work to achieve.

HARD WORK TO MAKE THE TEAM THE BEST

Good teams don't just happen. They need a great deal of work to achieve both high motivation from the members, and high performance and results from the team as a whole. This was very apparent when I studied the Red Arrows. Effort was made to ensure every member felt part of the team and regular reviews corrected mistakes in performance. This was achieved by a briefing before the flight, followed by a debriefing after the flight. These were to keep the team on target to achieve their overall goal – to be ready with a new display each May. (Performance was not originally mentioned by Woodcock, but he has since added 'standards'.)

Performance was an issue for writer Hackman (1987) in that he tries to explain why some groups perform better than others by suggesting that success is a joint function of three activities:

- the level of *effort* group members put in collectively in carrying out the task;

- the amount of *knowledge and skill* members bring to the team task;

- the appropriateness of the *performance strategies* or procedures used by the team in its work to achieve the task.

Each of these are relevant here. Knowledge and skill are demonstrated through both the flying test and the ability to get on with the other team members. These are both taken into account in the recruitment procedure and in the fact that the team choose the new members. Other organisations can change to accommodate this. Performance strategies include the briefing and debriefing procedures, where team members are encouraged to highlight their own and each others' mistakes to learn.

Within the team there are Squadron Leaders and Flight Lieutenants. Yet there appeared to be no hierarchy because they operated as a team, so instead of calling the Team Leader 'Sir', which is the normal procedure, they called him 'Boss' as it was less formal. During feedback and monitoring performance, team members criticised the Boss when he had not done something right, just as they would each other. Again, this is something that other organisations can readily take on board.

The amount of effort put in by team members can also be a problem area for teams. For instance, a top team I worked with had someone who had recently been slightly demoted because it was felt he did not have the right abilities or gave enough effort for the new demands of the company. This was very demotivating, but he was given every encouragement to still feel part of the team. He attended team meetings, but made it quite clear that he was not willing to give any more effort than he thought appropriate. Today, he has accepted early retirement and left the company, and the top team are achieving market growth through innovative products.

Several factors can influence the amount of effort team members will expend on carrying out the overall task. For a start, to encourage high effort the task should be challenging, important to the organisation and 'owned' by the team when members give their feedback on how the team is performing. This is achieved by the Red Arrows in the following way.

The task is challenging because although the team is made up of good pilots, they have to learn to fly formation aerobatics – a new type of flying – and often in very close manoeuvres. Therefore, they have to develop their flying skills further to meet the task objectives. In organisations a team is often hampered from extending its skills because of functional limitations and people who think they know everything. To resolve this, the objective should be linked to stretching people by the task itself and its performance standard.

As we have seen, the task of performing public displays is important to the RAF for three reasons. The first is to raise the profile of the RAF worldwide, the second is to attract recruits and the third is to demonstrate the standards of performance expected by all personnel. Therefore, the pilots feel like ambassadors and proud to be doing the job. It is by stretching and developing their skills that personal effort is forthcoming. In particular there is a shared vision of the purpose and aims of the team in the context of the organisation, and each individual member understands and recognises their part in contributing to this. How many teams in organisations have a clear reason for their existence which is known not only to the team but also every individual in the organisation? When this happens, individual and team performance improves.

The size of the team can also affect the exchange of knowledge and effort. Too large a team can encourage loafing or frighten someone who is not used to working with so many people. This means that those who make the biggest contribution will exercise most influence and, by keeping the others out of the participation, may deprive the team of important knowledge and skills. A high performing team, on the other hand, has a synergistic effect when team members interact and learn from each other.

In addition, the task is 'owned' by the team and a system of feedback is set up to show how each member is performing. This is done through the debriefing meetings. So the standard of the task becomes the standard for every member as a team, therefore maximising the effort of members.

A second factor which affects effort is reward. Again, when the reward provides teams with challenging performance objectives and reinforces their achievement, effort will be higher. One of the rewards for the Red Arrows comes at the end of six months' hard training when the Commander in Chief informs them that they are ready to put on the red suits. Up until this time, they fly in the usual green flying suits, so for the new team members particularly, red suit day is very rewarding.

This special day is an acknowledgement of their hard work. Different rewards could be developed in organisations and they clearly don't have to be monetary. We need to think about how to reward people as part of the process of developing the team. Reward leads to a feeling of pride, a good feeling to be part of an acknowledged team. It is a sad truth that many people at work never have this feeling, yet it doesn't require much to find a reward to match the effort. Hackman backs this up when he argues that, where individuals do not value membership of the team, their investment of effort will be low. Therefore, reward for effort pays off.

In conclusion, two so-called 'building blocks' are missing when looking at high performing teams. These are:

• standard of performance; and

• a reward system.

In addition, the research was showing processes which were influencing these 'building blocks' or characteristics and they were not solid, always visible blocks. What were they?

DEVELOPING THE FEELING OF TEAMNESS

If you've ever worked in a successful team you will have experienced the feeling of belonging to something special and 'a pleasant place'. This feeling of teamness was very apparent with the Red Arrows. I explain it as a 'we-feeling' as team members use the words 'we' and 'us' most of the time.

This feeling of teamness arrives when everyone is clear of what the objective is and their part in achieving it. Although individuals are very different, they have similarities and find that belonging to the team is a rewarding experience. This teamness will differ in strength according to the individuals but a good description has been given by Tom Douglas when he wrote: 'Teams generate a climate of loyalty which stems from the acceptance of dependence on others to achieve a desired outcome.'

This trust and dependence was clearly visible with the Red Arrows, partially because their lives depended on it. In other organisations that type of pressure is not there, but the pressure to survive, to succeed and perform well is there today. How do you develop trust and appropriate leadership? Woodcock's theory doesn't fully answer this. How does this teamness feel? What does it look like? The team members describe in their own words how it feels. I asked the pilots to use words to describe their perception of their team. This is the list. You will notice that some words are repeated. The team is:

- dedicated
- a happy place
- a great working environment
- very much an open forum for ideas
- the best thing that happened to me
- professional
- dynamic

- honest
- original
- friendly
- happy
- fun
- highly professional
- well organised
- a model unit
- highly motivated
- good public relations for the UK and the RAF
- recognised as one of, if not the best, display teams
- honest
- happy
- reliable
- well matched
- more important than the individual
- the best I have experienced
- a challenging job
- good fun to be a part of
- a good ambassador
- very close-knit but not exclusive
- honest with each other
- always striving for perfection
- professional
- helpful
- close-knit
- humorous

- conscientious
- self-critical
- very professional
- well organised
- effective
- careful
- always well prepared
- good company
- professional
- hard working
- critical
- happy
- stable
- professional
- the best
- fun to be with
- dedicated
- always in search of perfection
- from a wide variety of backgrounds

How do you achieve this in your teams? Building blocks are not enough – there were other processes involved. More research was needed to explain how this team worked year after year, constantly trying to improve its performance and strive for excellence. Team roles, characteristics and building blocks were not answering these and other questions. A new model was needed.

4

Internal and External Processes

"If there's a way to do it better . . . find it."

Edison

After one year's research the new model for high performing teams looked like a chain with interlocking links (see
Figure 5). But it still wasn't complete. When studying a
high performing team such as the Red Arrows it is easy to
identify the external strategies. We know that a motivated
team is more likely when the team members are working
towards clear, understood goals which they have influenced and helped to develop. In fact, working with the
Red Arrows, this was very clearly an important process. Yet
it wasn't explaining their total commitment to achieving
those goals.

Within the visible strategy of setting clear objectives and
goals was the less visible process of identifying and linking
their personal goals and vision to the objective. In other
words, team members knew each other's personal goals
and the team enabled those to become part of the
process. Therefore, for a high performing team it isn't
enough for the team to set the team goals, other distrac-

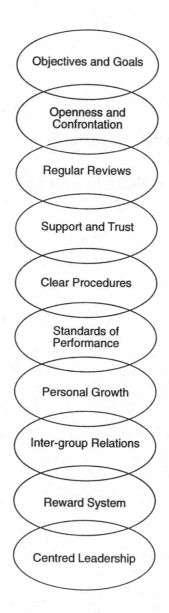

Figure 5 *External Strategy Chain*

tions and pressures often mean they forget or don't prioritise these goals. However, if team members incorporate their personal goals and vision for the team into the goals, they are more likely to achieve and even excel in achieving them.

These internal or less visible processes have been neglected by previous theories and are present in all the processes that are needed for a high performing team. They will be included here. Therefore, the model is made up of two chains – an external strategy chain and an internal process chain. Like the strategy chain, each internal process is linked and developing one will affect others. By working on both the external and internal processes, the team develops the property of synergy. Therefore, the research had to identify these internal processes which would be found in the Red Arrows and then test the theory to see if these processes were necessary in all teams.

More interviews and activities followed. I asked the pilots to use ten words to describe themselves, followed by ten words to describe the team. They were very aware of what they each brought to the team – and very honest. In all results the team was far greater than the sum of the pilots as individuals. Their personal descriptions contained both strengths and weaknesses, but the team had only strengths.

Here are some examples of what they said.

I am:

- determined
- sociable
- hard working
- a perfectionist
- not innovative
- short fused
- diligent
- sensitive

- self-critical
- humorous
- sometimes frustrated
- overweight

The team is:

- professional
- happy
- effective
- humorous
- good fun to be a part of
- always striving for perfection
- honest
- the best
- highly motivated
- the best thing that happened to me

The team also had the ability to give the members something they wouldn't have on their own. What do you take from your team? In organisations we still perceive a team as a group of individuals who share the work. But we need also to identify what the team gives its members and that has to be something members value.

The external process of being open and confronting mistakes was significant to the team, and it was possible because the members also included the internal process of having the right self-esteem and communicating in an assertive way. Self-esteem is the combination of whom we are and whom we would like to be. If the gap between these two is too wide, we fall down the middle and behave either aggressively or passively, letting people take advantage. When who we are and who we would like to be is not too far apart, our self-esteem is healthy and we can be effective in a team. In the case of the Red Arrows, team members actively developed their self-esteem which came from feedback from other team members and through their openness with each other. This internal process was linked to the external process of openness. Therefore, two chains were emerging – an external, or strategic, process chain and an internal process chain.

Teams need to develop both these chains of linked processes. The theory for high performing teams now looks like two chains and by working on both synergy develops and this enables the team to achieve far more. I decided to call the theory that emerged the 'synergy chain process'.

The external, strategic processes were defined first, while to identify the internal processes took longer. However, back in the UK a new Team Leader had joined the Red Arrows, along with three new pilots. It was this new team which we were going to film for the video and this gave me the opportunity to complete the identity of the internal process chain. It took several months of observing the team and another trip to Cyprus where the filming was completed, before the second chain was complete.

COMPLETING THE SECOND CHAIN – YEAR TWO

In a snow-covered winter, the first filming began. The three new pilots and new Team Leader were alone, working together. These pilots were capable young men, used to leading their own squadrons for front line missions. Yet close formation aerobatic flying was totally new to them, and it was up to the Team Leader to develop their flying skills and confidence to tackle this new challenge.

At this stage, the Team Leader took most of the decisions and did most of the talking. The new pilots listened and practised. Objectives were simple and daily, and based on developing the new pilots' skills and their trust in the

Team Leader. The four flew together with the boss in control and almost no involvement in planning by the new team members.

A few weeks later we returned to see a very different stage in the team process. Now seven of the nine pilots were working together, and there was much more input from the second and third years' team members. Experimentation had begun with ideas for new manoeuvres and involvement coming from the whole team, including the Team Leader. The debriefs were sometimes very lively, with the new pilots quieter than the rest, but criticism was part of the learning process and not threatening. If tension arose, the experienced pilots joked and released the tension with laughter. The new display was evolving and the team were working well together.

A process chain was developing – the *how* part of the chain was becoming clear. There were two chains emerging and it appeared that synergy was horizontal as well as vertical (see Figure 6, simplified). For example, the strategy chain of clear procedures was developing through the process chain of team involvement and innovation. In addition, the process links couldn't be separated from each other; for example, involvement and innovation couldn't be separated from self awareness and confidence, and so working on one affected the others – as did the strategy chain.

The next time we visited the air base it was early spring and the team were consolidating their input into a new display. Now the synchro pair were beginning to come back into the team, having been off developing and practising their input into the display. It was noticeable that the new pilots were now participating more in the debriefs and with ideas. The day was far more dynamic for everyone. The confidence of the new pilots had grown and the new Team Leader had gained the trust of all team members with his consistency. His style was very different to that of the past Team Leader, but by working on each chain of the synergy chain process his team were performing well. The display was coming together and looked very

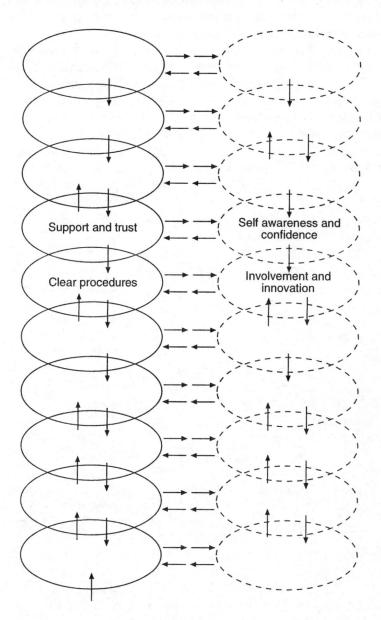

Figure 6 *How synergy flows*

different from the previous year. He had had to follow a well-respected Team Leader and it wasn't going to be easy. The results would be tested in Cyprus where the new display would be finally polished.

I visited Cyprus at the end of this final stage. The film crew were to film on what was hoped to be Red Suit Day. This is when the Commander in Chief decides the display is good enough to go public – but there is no guarantee that it will happen on the planned day. To our dismay we woke to find it raining! But the film crew were ready and we hoped it would not prevent the decision being made. The team did a practice sortie and we tried to find a good spot to do the filming. This year's display was faster and even more exciting to watch than the previous year's, but safety was paramount. Tapping into the innovation of all team members had produced a challenging show.

The tension was incredible. I had never seen these individuals, whom I had come to know well, so anxious. The pressure was rubbing off on to some of us. The sortie went well, the planes landed and even the rain had stopped. The Commander gave his debrief with us still filming. The atmosphere was electric. He went through the display, commenting on some of the manoeuvres, emphasising the need to watch the line crowd and praising some of the innovative moves. Finally, he said the words: 'The display is excellent, well done John, I now want you to put your red suits on.' They were ready.

Having put their red suits on for the first time that year, we caught the exciting moment by asking the team members how they felt. The consensus comment was 'relief'. A couple of hours later, the tension had gone and the team were partying. The process chain was complete (see Figure 7). The two years had resulted in a new theory on teams, concentrating on performance, showing that teams need to concentrate on both the what and how (or external and internal processes); that team members have to give and take from the team; and that the Team Leader's role is to work through these processes. The model now looked like two chains, each with ten links. To develop synergy and improve performance the chains are developed together – thus becoming one (see Figure 8).

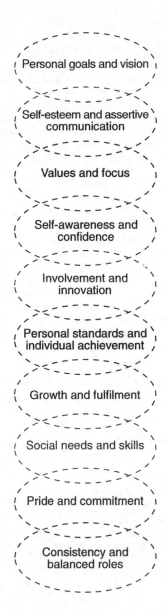

Figure 7 *Internal Process Chain*

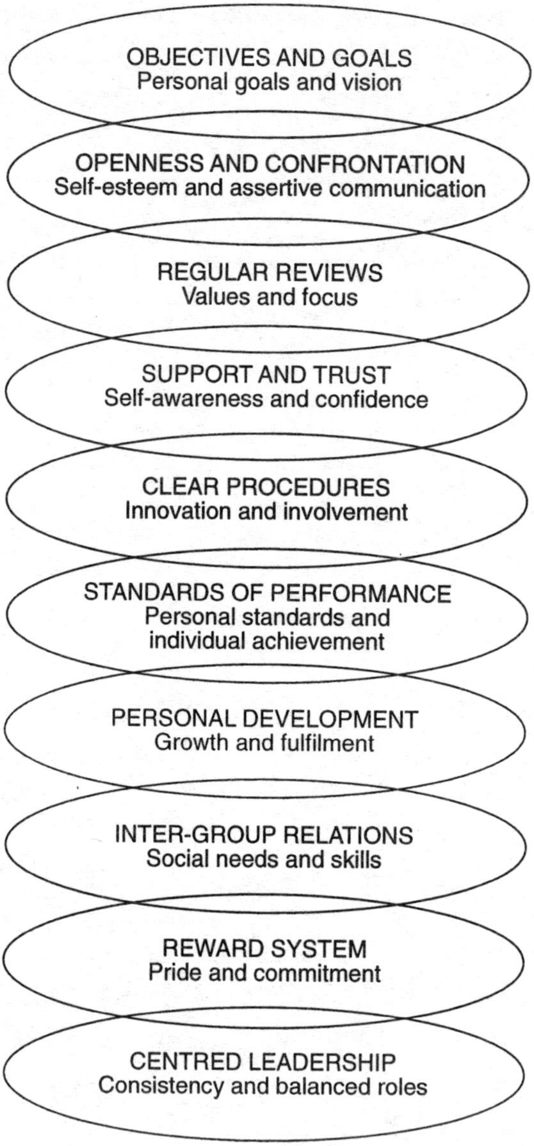

OBJECTIVES AND GOALS
Personal goals and vision

OPENNESS AND CONFRONTATION
Self-esteem and assertive communication

REGULAR REVIEWS
Values and focus

SUPPORT AND TRUST
Self-awareness and confidence

CLEAR PROCEDURES
Innovation and involvement

STANDARDS OF PERFORMANCE
Personal standards and
individual achievement

PERSONAL DEVELOPMENT
Growth and fulfilment

INTER-GROUP RELATIONS
Social needs and skills

REWARD SYSTEM
Pride and commitment

CENTRED LEADERSHIP
Consistency and balanced roles

Figure 8 *The Synergy Chain Process*

The challenge for the Reds was to keep striving for the perfect display throughout the season; the challenge for me was to test the theory with a couple of very different organisations.

The following case studies demonstrate the results.

BACK IN THE UK

Case Study 1

In this organisation the culture was based on individual power. I was working with a regional office of five people who were trying to establish a team in their office. However, they had some serious problems to overcome, including a head office where the culture was totally the opposite of teams. A colleague had once described his environment as somewhere 'If you have a heart attack, you're a hero; and if you have a nervous breakdown, you're a failure'.

The top man from head office spoke at the official opening of the regional branch, which I attended with a mixture of people from business, politics and public organisations. In his speech, he talked about some of the changes the organisation was tackling because of government legislation and said that his job was to make it as difficult as possible for public sector organisations going through these changes – which for me showed a negative way of dealing with change.

The regional office was headed up by a pleasant man close to retirement who saw his position as a relatively easy life until he retired. The last thing he wanted was to face up to serious issues. This enabled his second in command, a strong self-interested individual who was motivated totally by personal power, to do things no one knew about. He was ambitious and believed he should be running the office.

The office manager and secretary were considered beneath him, but they could see the games he played with people. In the middle was an officer whom he tolerated, but dismissed her as a problem because she was a woman. Against this unpromising background I began working with them.

Day one had not been easy. People had arrived with misconceptions of what the programme would be like. This was also reinforced by a culture that didn't encourage openness and so, to begin with, people held back. In addition, the team had no clear direction, objectives or goals. There was an element of waiting to see if these would come from head office. Therefore, to begin we looked at how the team members could decide and develop their own objectives and goals. This included identifying and incorporating their own personal goals. The process enables the team to start opening up and I ensured that each team member, including number two, told the team exactly what they wanted to achieve.

The team leader realised that his easy life didn't mean ignoring the personal goals of the rest of the team. Not only did he have to deal with a power-hungry number two, he discovered the importance of the other team members' needs, which included more involvement and responsibility. Clarifying the objectives was also helped when looking at setting up a way of regularly reviewing the objectives and goals as the process concentrated on what to focus on and how to incorporate values. This brought the team closer and moved them forward in identifying what to concentrate on.

On the second day everyone began to open up and participate more. Their scepticism had vanished and they began to pull together. There was even a 'buzz' in the afternoon as the team began to feel they could succeed. After three days the team had worked on the links and were ready to go it alone.

A couple of months later, I returned to find a dynamic team, pulling together in the same direction. Their individual performance had improved and the team as a whole were making their mark.

Today, the team are achieving and working together to help the individuals they serve. They are a committed team with strong ideas and a belief in serving the public. That is except for the number two man. The openness became his downfall. People can't use coercive power in an open environment. He resigned after the branch found out he'd been dishonest. This highlights the need to sometimes replace team members.

One of the Team Leaders of the Reds said 'You are as strong as your weakest link'. He had to get rid of a pilot who didn't come up to the expected performance. The decision was taken by the team and he implemented it. Don't be afraid of doing this – it happens in the best teams. Don't accept less than the standard of performance required. By not taking this stance, you are letting the team down.

Case Study 2

The second organisation was a medium sized manufacturing company operating in a high-tech and fast changing market. A visit clarified that the top team of directors and senior managers needed to develop as a high performing team to utilise the opportunities the company had generated. This was put on hold following a restructuring which had caused some difficult internal politics. Therefore it was decided that the work would go ahead with the top sales team instead as they had an urgent problem.

The sales team was made up of experienced men who had been disrupted by a newcomer they decided they did not respect. He had been recruited by the managing director as sales director (designate). This man arrived with a bit of a negative reputation in the industry. His characteristic was to rush around, interfere and leave, rush on to another thing and not follow through others. He had upset many people in the company but the MD wanted him to lead the sales team. My task was to try and make them a high performing team.

Working through both the strategy and process chains individuals were truly open with each other. It became clear that the new sales director suffered from low self-esteem which led to an inconsistent leadership style. His rushing around – being seen to be busy – gave him a feeling of importance to compensate. We spent some time exploring the process links. The Reds were able to be open with each other because they had the right balance of self-esteem and used assertive communication, while their trust in each other came from growing more aware of themselves as individuals.

The sales director was surprised to hear the other team members appreciate his ability to walk into a room of people and generate interest in the company's products. He, in turn, began to move his focus from himself to the other team members, and discover their skills and experience.

Today, the team are going from strength to strength, with worldwide sales being generated from a team who are working together based on trust. Together they are achieving high performance. Their success has resulted in the company splitting into two strategic business units – one for international sales and the other for UK end users.

Soon after, the top team went through the programme. The managing director was a visionary and, although he knew where he wanted to go, the rest of the team were not always so clear about the future and where they fitted in. This future was clearly defined, and each team member identified the objectives and goals necessary to achieve it. The programme also helped them realise that a top team is more than 'functional heads' and instead we spent time looking at the strengths of the team as individuals. These were then matched to their objectives, which led to one team member changing his role and concentrating on a part of the business he was better able to manage. This team member became much happier and the whole team were clear for the first time about where they were going.

This has resulted, a year later, in innovative products that have turned the company around. As the MD said: 'Ninety per cent of our equipment revenues now come from products that didn't exist two years ago. . .Export sales have more than doubled and will grow strongly into the future.'

Case studies 1 and 2 show that you may have to remove someone, or you may have to develop the team and some of the individuals, but no team is perfect, not even the Reds. There are sometimes team members who rub others up the wrong way – but the team is what holds them together and by working on the links in the synergy chain process, performance is enhanced.

Case Study 3

The third organisation was a national firm of chartered accountants. The senior partner wanted to develop a group of accountants, with mixed experience and qualifications, into a team to improve the way clients were looked after and new business was generated. There were three main weaknesses the team members had to address: What are we supposed to do; How can we inter-relate with others who up until now have not perceived us as a team; and how does a Team Leader, who was used to being 'one of the girls', change her role, and gain respect and acknowledgement from her new peers?

The team already had a good amount of trust between each other. We began with the issue of objectives and goals. These were developed alongside their personal goals and vision. The team quickly realised that *they* must set these and 'own' them. This they did.

We then tackled the issue of intergroup relations. Others in the company tended to see the individuals as 'spare hands' and they had to stop this. By concentrating on the social skills of understanding others and our own needs and assertive communication, this issue was resolved by the team members recognising that they had to change their perception of themselves before others would. It meant that the team would have to change its behaviour with other groups in the company and acknowledge their own needs. This was enhanced when we worked on the links for establishing a reward system which would give pride and ownership to their success. As one team member said: 'Having attended the programme, I feel our team is developing a good perception within the office as a whole. For me personally, I am now aware of not only my own needs but also the needs of my fellow team members.'

The final issue was with the new Team Leader. We worked at identifying her roles, and how to balance them and be consistent. This included her actions with the team members and other groups in the company.

Today, the team is working well, and the Team Leader has quickly gained the respect and trust of both her team and colleagues. In addition, they are innovative in customer care, and have been recognised as performing well by their peers and senior partners.

The theory worked for these three organisations – even under difficult circumstances. Today, it is working with boards of directors, senior management teams and employee teams. We will now explore the synergy chain process in more depth and understand how it works, and, in particular, how it can work for you.

PART II

OBJECTIVES AND GOALS
Personal goals and vision

OPENNESS AND CONFRONTATION
Self-esteem and assertive communication

REGULAR REVIEWS
Values and focus

SUPPORT AND TRUST
Self-awareness and confidence

CLEAR PROCEDURES
Innovation and involvement

STANDARDS OF PERFORMANCE
Personal standards and
individual achievement

PERSONAL DEVELOPMENT
Growth and fulfilment

INTER-GROUP RELATIONS
Social needs and skills

REWARD SYSTEM
Pride and commitment

CENTRED LEADERSHIP
Consistency and balanced roles

The Synergy Chain Process

5

The Synergy Chain Process

"A race horse that can run a mile a few seconds faster is worth twice as much. That little extra proves to be the greatest value."

John D Hess

From two years' work this new theory on teams has emerged and its results are shown to enhance performance – produce that bit extra in a team. It is worth recapping on the theory here, before looking at each link in the chain in detail. The synergy chain is made up of ten links which overlap each other. This means that if you are developing one link, you inevitably develop others in some way.

The difference with this theory is that each link has an external, strategy process and an internal, less visible process. The aim is to develop the external, strategy processes and the internal, less visible processes together. It is through developing BOTH in each link that synergy is created. In addition, by working on all the links you will see how they affect each other and how 'super-synergy' emerges. Therefore, although synergy means 1 + 1 = 3, with high performing teams 1 + 1 can equal 3000 or even more.

The essence of synergy is to value the differences in the

team and build on the strengths through working on each link in the chain. It then becomes creative and exciting for team members, while at the same time their performance is at its full potential. Once people have experienced this synergy in a team, they will never accept less. Therefore, it is possible to have a chain effect in the organisation. However, the best results have occurred when the board, management and employees all go through this process.

Finally, there is no hierarchy of links; each is valued equally. On completion, the chain is joined up, like a bracelet. It is the role of all team members, but particularly the Team Leader to ensure that each link is maintained and constantly strengthened.

To examine this further, I'm going to break up this synergy chain into individual parts so you can see how it works and how you can use it in your organisation. For each link, the strategic process is stated first, with the internal process in italics.

1

Clear objectives and mutual goals identified and agreed by the team

Personal goals and vision of each individual

You have to decide what you want before you can achieve something. For many teams it is assumed that the objectives are known and committed to. This is often the first weak link in the team. You have to visualise the success – the outcome – see it in your mind, feel it, experience it.

'What I have here are nine very, very talented pilots and some very, very talented engineers . . . everyone can see the goal is outside every day. The aeroplanes sit on the line and they see them fly. The team is very much aware of what it is trying to achieve and they see the results.' Team Leader

Many of the organisations I have worked with thought they knew their goals and assumed everyone else knew them too. The other fault is to wait for the goals and objectives to come from above. This happened in two of the examples we have just looked at in the previous chapter. The team has to make a decision on its own objectives and goals.

So, one of the first things the team does is agree the objectives and goals together. This does not mean your everyday goals only; they should include long-term objectives too. An approach is to identify within a team those areas which need priority attention to contribute best to the overall organisation objectives and to achieve specific work goals successfully. Then set performance targets and objectives in each area which will keep team members on course to achieve the goals successfully.

Measuring performance is the next step, to see whether what you set out to achieve is accomplished. Finally, using the results of monitoring by feedback to tell people what they have achieved and set new goals, or assess why goals were not achieved, take action to ensure future success. Wouldn't everything be great if it were as straightforward as this all the time? Of course it isn't. Therefore, we need to look at the process link to help.

Included here should be the values of the team, as people have to accept that the objectives and goals are worth striving for. Secondly, in agreeing the team goals, the team members should also identify their own personal objectives and goals. This means 'an aim we are striving to attain'. For the Red Arrows the team goal was to have a new display ready for presenting to the general public in time for the summer season. The personal goals included being technically competent to fly to the best of their ability so as not to let the rest of the team down. This personal goal was high up on the list for most of the members.

But there were other personal goals which included learning how to deal with the public. During their three years as a team member, the pilots have to see hundreds of people visiting the base. They also do TV appearances and present money to charities and hospitals raised through the Red Arrows Trust Fund. These pilots and the team manager are suddenly public figures and ambassadors for the RAF, involving handshaking, interviews and answering the same questions over and over. This wasn't easy for many of the team members, and by becoming one of their personal goals it became challenging and part of their new job. It is therefore important to know the personal goals of the individuals because they will help achieve the team goal by aligning them with the organisation's goals.

Many teams discuss the team goals, but not the individual goals. This can even include learning to be a better team player, as one of the Reds discovered.

> 'I wanted to be a better team player, to feel part of the way a small group of people work together to a clear target. It's not just the air crew, the ground crew have a clear objective because they want to get nine aeroplanes in the air at the same time. You have to make decisions, do something and present the information to the rest of the people.' Pilot

These personal goals and vision affect the performance of individual team members. When people feel helpless or hopeless and lose sight of their personal goals, or feel that no matter what they do, they won't achieve their goals – they won't. It is these beliefs that freeze us and prevent us from achieving our goals – not the fact that the team is short of resources. You can work around that.

You have to know what you want, believe you can achieve and then you have something to move towards. This needs to be done for both personal and team goals. Therefore, having a clear team objective and goals which incorporate personal goals and achievements is the first process step in achieving high performing teams. Ask each individual what they personally desire to achieve in the team as well as identifying the team goals. Then add a 'synergy' element by identifying what the team can achieve which individual members could not achieve on their own. The whole team should develop the goals and this leads to commitment. The Team Leader should clarify the goals at every step of the journey in terms of what the team will do – not how the team will achieve it. The team members will decide how.

In addition to ensuring consistent performance, setting objectives has a motivational value as team members will have a clearer sense of purpose and see how their work fits into the larger context. It is also a way of bringing continuous improvement in work, and gives a sense of achievement and aspiration. Working on these links is also setting the groundwork for team members being more open with each other and leads to the second link in the chain.

To summarise this first link, the key points are:

- don't assume everyone knows the goals and is committed to them;

- together decide the team's objectives and goals;

- include the team members' individual goals and incorporate those into the team goals.

2

Openness and confrontation to enable the team to learn from mistakes

Self-esteem and assertive communication

To achieve high performance, teams need to share information, ideas and even problems with each other. Team members do this openly, without fear of retaliation. Instead of avoiding unpleasant or delicate issues, they confront them openly. This is an on-going process of monitoring and feedback about the team's task and individual performance.

We live in a society where keeping your ideas and feelings to yourself is still common. You have to break down this barrier in a team, say what you want and feel in a way which doesn't trample over others. Expressing opinions and ideas openly may be difficult for some, but if you try to stop people stating their views in order to suppress differences of opinions, you'll take away the incentive to get really involved with the team's work.

Feedback is not always easy, and requires assertive communication and response. In other words, the feedback must not be a personal attack, but factual and accepted with agreement on what can be done to improve performance.

Accepting criticism is never easy, but it was a daily process with the Reds, regardless of rank. After every sortie, including displays in the summer, the Reds spend 10 to 15 minutes discussing the flight and the manoeuvres, and giving feedback to each other on how they performed and what needs to be corrected.

'The total openness at the debriefs is vital. Even the Team Leader has to accept this. We pay respect to his status, of course, but you cannot back off from saying "you did that wrong" because he is senior to you. It is the confidence in the team which allows them to say it to you and you accept the criticism.' Pilot

---

Therefore confidence plays an important part in developing openness. Playwright Vaclav Havel addressed the people of Czechoslovakia on New Year's Day in 1990 by saying: 'Only a person (or a nation) self-confident in the best sense of the word is capable of listening to the voice of others and accepting them as equal to oneself.'

Confident and assertive communication comes from having a healthy feeling of self – or self-esteem. This only happens when the two views we have of ourselves and the person we'd like to be are comfortably close. If these two are far apart, a person dislikes himself and has low self-esteem. This leads to either aggressive or passive communication, both of which are problematic in being open and confronting issues.

A team member who is not being open but aggressive, or shies away from confronting issues, will be doing him or herself and the team a disservice, and performance will be below its potential. Information will be necessary for the team to operate, but it must be quality information rather than quantity. The information must be relevant to the team and aid understanding. Therefore, the information may be controversial or confrontational, but it is more important that team members understand how each member is affected by the information.

> 'We have good days and we have bad days. As a team, as we go through the season we get stronger because of that. And all of us are encouraged to highlight our own mistakes and highlight each other's mistakes.'
> Pilot

Feedback is part of this openness, and must involve both actively seeking it and listening, taking it on board and acting on it. This way, the openness becomes a positive way of learning how to improve each team member's performance.

> 'When you make a mistake, when you come to a debrief, you've only got so many hours in the day. You've got three sorties to get in. You actually haven't got time to flog it to death. You've got to put your hand up and say, that was me who did that wrong. That way, you can get on to the next thing and start learning.' Pilot

If a team member is not listening and acting on feedback, other members will feel frustrated, angry and then give up saying anything. The Team Leader has an important role here and must:

- get to know the individuals in the team – their values and what motivates them;
- ensure everyone knows what is expected of them, discuss the goals and any changes with team members, rather than spring things on them;
- show individuals that their contribution is valued;
- give feedback about performance regularly – not just at appraisal time.

Being open and confronting issues also means revealing yourself. This is easy when you are with friends – but what about when you are with the team you work with?

Joseph Luft and Harrington Ingham developed an interesting diagram to identify four kinds of information about yourself which is relevant here (see Figure 9). It is a window with four panes – each representing you as you relate to others. The open pane includes all the things you know and don't mind sharing with others. Obviously the more you know a person, the more you reveal. The blind pane includes all that other people see in you, but you cannot see yourself. You may think you are a good communicator, but others may see you as abrasive or bossy. It is through feedback that this pane becomes open and we grow.

The hidden pane represents your secrets, things you choose not to reveal. Everyone has them and you have control of this pane. The unknown pane is everything both you and others are to learn about yourself. It's the chapters yet to be written – the window pane of discovery and challenge.

A high performing team opens up this window by using self-disclosure. This involves sharing both facts and feelings about things which are relative to the team. It isn't easy for many and does involve risk to oneself or a feeling of being threatened by another. However, if this openness is part of the regular feedback procedure it becomes part of the normal way of doing things. In the case of the Reds, the debrief session was a formal way of doing this and although it could get quite strong, it never felt threatening to the team members.

If a team is to be successful, its members must be able to state their views about each other and air differences without fear of ridicule or retaliation. Effective teams at all levels shouldn't avoid delicate or unpleasant issues, but confront them honestly. Positive handling of conflict entails looking for solutions – not for somewhere or someone to blame. It means avoiding turning confrontations into win/lose situations instead of working to win/win outcomes. Seeking compromise will be high on the agenda – as long as the compromise doesn't mean failing to achieve the team's goals.

As this openness increases, so does the trust and ability to deal with any conflict situation. Therefore it is part of the Team Leader's role to develop openness, which in turn develops trust. This cannot be forced; it has to be encour-

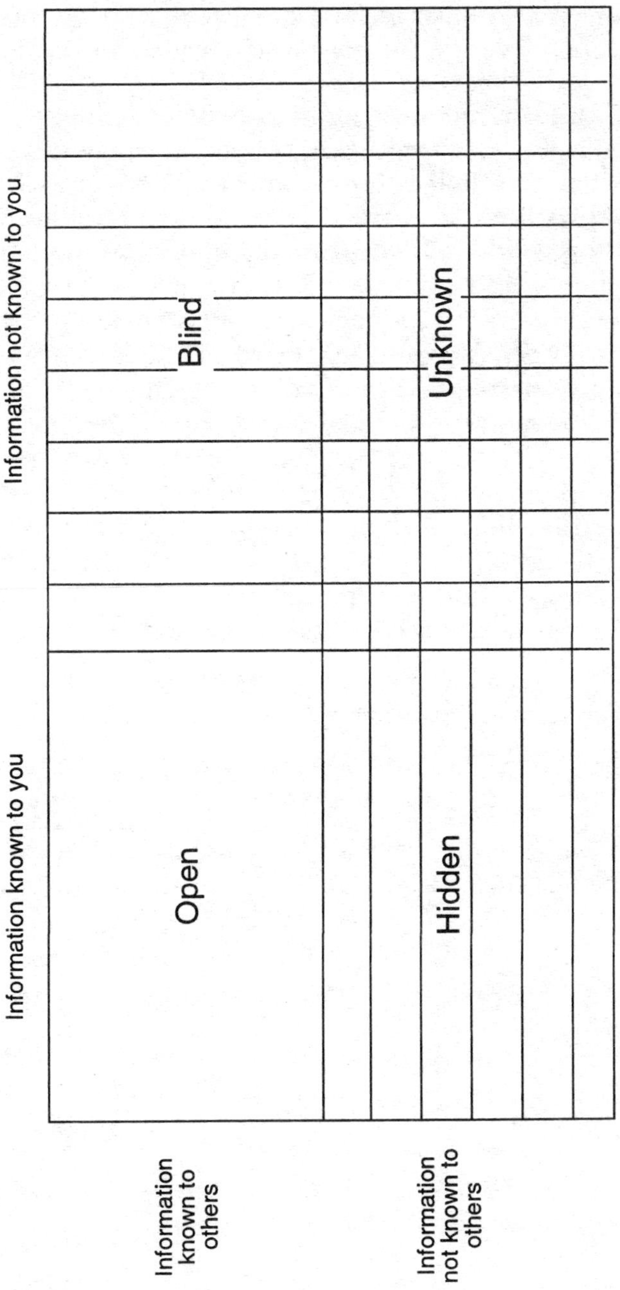

Figure 9 *Johari Window*

aged and seen as part of the natural procedure of working as a team. It also must include the leader who should seek and accept feedback on his or her leadership or performance.

Ask each team member to disclose the personal strengths and weaknesses of everyone. Encourage each team member to say what they find helpful about that person as well as what annoys them about that person. Then together agree what action would help the team to continue being open.

Handling – and even at times encouraging – the open expression of critical judgements, differing views and conflicting attitudes is part of teamwork. The more you reveal yourself to others, the more you will learn about yourself. It can be exciting and satisfying to open these window panes – but it can also be painful and involves risk. To minimise this risk, the team must make this part of their regular reviewing process, whereby the reviews become learning situations. This way, the openness is part of that learning process and not threatening.

To summarise this second link, the key points are:

- teams have to be open and honest with each other to share information and give feedback;

- honest feedback should be used to learn from situations, not for a personal attack;

- when we do this we learn more about ourselves and build a healthy self-esteem.

3

Regular reviews to consistently learn

Values and focus

Two of the most basic processes in achieving goals as a team are:

- the sharing of needed information, ideas and even problems among the group; and

- the ongoing process of monitoring and giving feedback about tasks and performance.

This is done through regular reviews which become part of the procedures. You can also see how this is inextricably attached to link 2. Regular reviews are opportunities to be open and highlight what is working, what isn't working and why, and how to improve both individual and team performance.

The Reds did this by following a routine aimed to enhance performance. They involved a briefing to establish the goals for that sortie, doing the sortie and debriefing afterwards or having regular reviews to identify the mistakes and rectify them next time. This usually occurs three times a day, particularly nearer the start of the season, to get the display as nearly perfect as possible.

Mistakes are seen as part of the natural learning process, not an excuse to scold – an opportunity many organisations still need to realise.

> 'You learn that those mistakes are not the be all and end all, and that you can learn from them. You must not be afraid of making mistakes, just put them behind you and try not to repeat them. If you are afraid of making mistakes you will never get any better.' Pilot

Therefore these reviews concentrate on information about performance which should lead to action to maintain or improve performance. How can the team incorporate regular reviews into the way the members work together?

As the members of the team build trust they can also start to ask how they are feeling about things. This doesn't mean a floodgate of emotions pours out – it enables team members to express their feelings in a safe environment. They can then be resolved and put behind them. This will lead to team members being able to concentrate on their performance without being distracted.

This links with openness, and will only work if all team members are honest with each other and themselves. Done correctly and regularly reviews are seen as constructive and not threatening. This process enables the Red Arrows team members to strive for high standards of performance which do not stop once the public displays commence. During the summer the team still have briefing meetings followed by the debrief after the display. For the public who see it, the display will be exciting and perfect flying – but for some team members there is still a tiny error to get right.

> 'The six months of the winter we try to develop and structure a display, and try to make it as near perfect as we can. The important thing is when we have been cleared to do the new public display we continue to always strive to make it perfect. If you stop striving for that level of perfection, you will never get any better. We could say "We're the Red Arrows, we're great", but what good does that do? We make time to review after the show and that leads to the open discussions about

what things have not worked. Time is not wasted doing this because people will openly admit they are out of position at a particular time. Next time they will make the effort to put it right. This whole trust element revolves around knowing what is expected of you and that every team member will strive to achieve it.' Pilot

The underlying processes here are to identify your values and work towards the focused goal. Values are things which are important to you. It is through self-awareness that you can examine and recognise your values. What do you care about? What makes your life at work meaningful? What is most important to you?

We each have a natural and individual hierarchy of values, and they should be shared with the team. Then together you can decide how the important values can be incorporated into the goals of the team and taken into account in the regular reviews. For the Reds, providing an exciting display for the public makes their work meaningful. But at the same time, the public's safety is also an important value. Therefore, in the reviews they concentrate on enhancing their performance to make it exciting, while keeping the display at a safe distance from the crowd line. Balancing these two values is part of their regular reviews.

These reviews involve all team members. Regular reviews don't just provide a vehicle for learning from experience, they should also motivate the members in seeing what's going on and provide an opportunity for redefining roles or resetting objectives if necessary. The purpose of feedback, then, is two-fold. Motivational feedback tells a person that good performance has been noticed and gives recognition for it, so helping their confidence and motivating them to repeat the good performance in the future. Motivational feedback is given immediately after the performance.

Developmental feedback tells a person what needs to be done better next time and should be given in particular just before the next performance, so that the member is helped and encouraged to do things better the next time. This feedback is seen as support rather than criticism. Many managers tend to give developmental feedback only at such times as appraisal or performance review and, as a result, people justifiably complain that they did not realise they could be doing the job better. The Red Arrows do this three times a day as part of their regular reviews.

Another often cited complaint is that people never hear motivational feedback – only criticism when things go wrong. It is important that feedback is both positive as well as negative. If someone has done well, they should be told. It is through feedback – getting the reactions of others – that we learn, improving individual competence and achievement.

We are now focusing on both what to do and how to do it. It is our focused efforts which achieve the most. We focus through having regular reviews which are there to enhance the performance of team members. It is this regular focusing on performance that ensures the Red Arrows maintain their high standards year after year and with different teams. It is through these focused regular reviews that team members develop trust and this takes us to the next link.

To summarise this third link, the key points are:

- regular reviews enable the team to keep on track and ensure that performance is enhanced;

- incorporated into these should be the values important to the team;

- always keep the main objective in mind – keep focused.

4

Total trust and support leads to commitment and communication based on openness

Self-awareness and confidence

Tom Peters recently wrote: 'Obviously, we can no longer succeed with a steep hierarchy in place. The flat organisation alternative demands much more delegation of authority to the front line. That is, "we" must learn to trust "them". And we, in turn, will only trust them when they trust us. This reciprocal arrangement, the basis of all healthy relationships, must become the cornerstone of tomorrow's adaptive enterprise.' This, I believe, is the most important statement ever written by Peters. Can I trust the organisation to back up their commitments? Can I trust the team to perform when needed? Do the team members support each other? Trust is the glue that holds the team together.

An organisation becomes trustworthy only as the individuals in it become trustworthy. Therefore if the organisation is to develop trust it must take on board fully these words by Gandhi: 'We must become the change we seek in the world.' If managers and directors are serious about developing teams in their organisations, they must become trustworthy and work as teams themselves. All too often, there is a push in this direction, and then a manager or director will say or do something which contradicts any trust. When this happens, people become sceptical and eventually don't believe what they hear any more. This becomes particularly apparent when the organisation is trying to change.

In contrast, the Reds, in particular the Team Leader, developed trust by their consistent behaviour, words and actions. This was the first link I identified in the Red Arrows. Sceptics may argue that trust is expected in a team whose job is dangerous. When I mentioned this to the team members, they replied that they wouldn't do the job if it was dangerous. In fact, this process takes away danger as far as possible. During the display, two pilots break off, the synchro pair, and return with the most spectacular fast

> 'He has got to have 100 per cent trust in me and if he does not have that he can't commit himself to some of the things we do, and therefore our performance would be less than perfect and could easily result in an accident. It is the same for me because he is the guy who has to miss me. It amounts to us both having confidence in each other's ability.' Synchro Leader speaking of his partner

flying, crossing each other in the air, leaving crowds breathless.

At work we have to trust people though sceptics put up walls because they don't know how to do it.

What do we mean by trust and support? Trust must imply being allowed to get on with a job on the understanding that the individual will do it the best way they know how. Do you trust your colleagues? Do you trust your boss? If not, why not? Trust takes time to achieve – but can be destroyed in seconds. So, how do you build trust?

To inspire trust it is necessary to look at your own character – who you are, what you are and your competence – what you can do. Trust is established over time, and comes from both reliability and consistency. The Team Leader sets the example by:

- being open and honest in facing problems;

- having high personal and team standards;

- being true to beliefs and values;

- confronting issues as they arise;

- using delegation to encourage development and achievement, not just to reduce the workload;

- being accessible and receptive;

- taking responsibility and using judgement;

- giving trust and support to team members, and others outside the core team;

- establishing clear goals and objectives with the team for effective work practices.

The most effective way of doing this is through team members getting to know each other, by being open and talking about the objectives and goals, the required standards and reviewing how it's going. You will find that you can achieve more when there is trust. One of the Reds demonstrates this:

'We build up and develop an awful lot of trust between the guys as we work together. The whole display is based on the fact that we can do certain things because we trust one another. When you are in the sky you have to know that when the plane next to you is supposed to do something, it will happen. So when you move your aeroplane around the sky, you know he is not going to be there and that everything is clear. You don't need to be checking up on him all the time – he has his job to do and you have yours. If it does not go the way it should, we come back to ground and talk about it in an honest and friendly manner, and find out what went wrong. It is not a session to be horrible to one another, it is just a chance to find why it did not work, so we can put it right next time.' Pilot

Studying the Reds it became clear that the team members built trust through understanding and trusting themselves, and that this confidence grew along with the trust in each other. To develop trust and support, team members need to develop the internal processes of self-awareness and confidence, and accept who they are.

Write 'I am' on a piece of paper and fill the rest of the sheet up with how you would describe yourself. This is how you see yourself – your self-concept. How many of these items are positive and how many are negative? Our self-concept is developed by the interactions, feedback and our interpretation of those interactions we have from our earliest childhood – our parents, teachers, friends, colleagues, bosses. For those people who sometimes made it difficult for us, the first thing we must do is forgive, which isn't always easy.

It is amazing how someone can say negative things which influence us for the rest of our lives if we allow them to. The parent or teacher who said we couldn't do something results in us never mastering a skill. This is called the 'self-fulfilling prophecy' and by forgiving the person who said it we can change things to prove them wrong. An ugly duckling can become a swan or someone who failed at school can end up with a PhD. The difference is they learn to believe in themselves and can in future concentrate on the positive feedback they hear.

Confidence comes from first trusting yourself – believing you can do a good job. What experiences have led you to become aware of both your strengths and weaknesses? What achievements are you proud of? Barbra Streisand once said: 'You have got to discover you, what you do, and trust it.' Once we trust ourselves we can start to trust others. Trust was developed in the Reds as they worked together, giving each other honest feedback. This feedback was not perceived as personally threatening, but constructive because they had self-awareness and confidence, and trusted each other.

> 'The whole thing relies on you trusting the person next to you to do the right thing at the right time, so you can concentrate on what you are doing, without any cross-checking. Therefore, extra effort and brain power is not wasted on what is already a highly concentrated role.' Pilot

Performance develops similarly to that of companies who have developed 'continuous improvement' and understand the supplier/customer chain in an organisation. For continuous improvement to thrive, there has to be trust.

Building trust was part of the procedures and practices the Reds undertook every day. We now need to look at the next link which is procedures, because trust also grows as team members become more involved in the day-to-day work of a team.

Before we do this, let's summarise the key points:

- trust takes time and is helped by being consistent;
- we can only trust others when we trust ourselves, so we need to be aware of ourselves;
- we have to be confident to believe we can do our job, then we must trust others to do theirs.

5

Procedures and practices which enhance team performance

Involvement and innovation

The procedures are the actions which take you forward and should maximise the synergy of the team – not be in place to justify the team or occur for the sake of it. Too often in organisations, procedures and practices stagnate innovation and restrict performance. Instead, the members of the team need to look at how they do things to enhance performance. The process to unlock this is to involve all team members and tap into their ideas and innovation as they grow and reach the standards required for the team.

During their three years as a Red Arrow, the flying position changes for team members and as the months progress confidence grows as well as skills, and pilots are given different tasks to achieve for the team as well as fly fast jets.

'My first year was on the wing, my second year was learning the role of synchro, my third year has meant me becoming the teacher. I found it quite daunting at first because there is nothing in terms of synchro work that you can learn from a book, there is nothing tangible, you have to teach it by mouth to ensure all the safety points are covered. There is nothing written down, no training manuals on how to do it and tailor it to the other guy.' Third Year Pilot

The internal processes here are involvement and bringing innovation to the team. How does the team determine its practices or agendas? How does it make decisions? How is the work co-ordinated? How does the team identify and make use of the strengths and resources in its team members? Is it through involving team members in these and other issues that innovation surfaces?

For the Reds the procedures begin when the team decides on the three new pilots for the following year. This is vital, and a lesson organisations should try to adopt. It means that you begin with barriers down and can commence working with the team straight away because you know the team picked you.

'We choose each other and that is hugely important. The personalities are therefore not grating against one another, and we are all willing to sit there and take the debriefs, which, especially in the first year, are hard because you are constantly being told you are wrong, but we try to make a joke out of it. You do need the personality to accept that as a new boy you will be treated as a new boy, although we are all very experienced pilots. They left jobs in high positions in the hierarchy of the normal squadron. They come here and have to run the coffee bar, and are told they are not very good all the time.' Pilot

It's vital everyone understands their role and their relationships with other team members. Think of a situation when the team is working well and achieving things. What is helping this? You will find that when the team are clear about what they are doing, when they are involved and using their own ideas, procedures enhance this. The new Team Leader involved the third year pilots:

'He calls in the older guys, we can call ourselves if you like, before the brief and he runs through what he is trying to do and tries to iron out any problems so that the brief comes across well, as opposed to disjointed with mistakes in it.' Third Year Pilot

This approach enables all team members to be involved. For instance, while observing the Reds, within weeks I saw first year pilots putting forward ideas for new manoeuvres and suggestions to develop the team confidently. Therefore, procedures should enhance the performance of individuals and the team as a whole.

Two procedures which constantly need looking at in organisations are meetings and how communication channels work. It is through getting people involved in these issues that innovative ideas develop to improve some of these procedures. This should also be done in the team, and by being open and trusting each other it becomes easier. At the same time, if standards are set they should include how these procedures operate. This way, procedures are not there to hamper, but to improve performance.

Maintaining these procedures is the responsibility of the whole team, but the Team Leader must ensure that everyone is involved. It is also up to the Team Leader to see that everyone is involved and committed to the standards set by the team to achieve their goals.

To summarise the fifth link, the key points are:

- look to improve procedures to make the team more innovative and effective;
- involvement is crucial;
- maintaining these procedures is the responsibility of the whole team.

6

Standards of performance for the team to aspire to

Personal standard for individual achievements

As well as setting out objectives and goals, the team members need to be clear about the standard they need to achieve. When working with teams I have found this to be an issue which can pull a team apart if there is a feeling that not everyone is working to the same required standard. This is usually because it hasn't been clarified. Once this standard is set, every team member must know it, and feel they can achieve it.

This links with personal development as each team member develops their ability to achieve the standard. Regular procedures should enable team members to be clear about the standard as well as work towards achieving it. By being open with each other, regular feedback will ensure that everyone works to this standard, as they should be told if team members are not performing to the required level. Therefore, the standards should be set by and 'owned' by the team members, and be part of why the team are working together.

> 'The team sets the standard. If my performance wasn't up to scratch, I would be told as well.' Team Leader

Like objectives and goals, team members should state what personal standards they want to achieve and these should become part of the overall standards of performance. By doing this, team members will constantly strive to ensure success. Some of the Reds said:

> 'Standing amongst your peers is important, so you work to get your own standard high, and you want the team to do well so getting myself performing well means the team will do well.'
> 'I try to do the best for myself and the team.'
> 'There is an ethos of the team to be perfect and we all have to strive towards that.' Pilots

If you think that all these pilots have to concentrate on is flying, you're wrong. Each has other work to do and if this is not of the required standard, things will start to go wrong. For example, if the pilots responsible for the routes and maps didn't work to the same standard, the team would arrive at venues late. This is carried through to the most mundane task. For example, one of the first year Reds has to look after the coffee bar and if the team were to run out of snacks, coffee or biscuits, the team member would be told very succinctly that he was not doing his job properly!

> 'It's your own personal responsibility to make sure your own particular area is absolutely watertight.' Pilot

What other areas of performance are affecting the team? One of the most important team members is Red 10 or the Team Manager. Although he doesn't fly one of the Hawks in the displays, he will be a pilot and have the rank of Squadron Leader. His work includes setting up all the displays for the summer, speaking at outside events and doing the commentary at the display. He is the 'front man' and the Red most people come into contact with. His job involves dealing with the general public as well as RAF personnel. He also has to set a standard of performance for himself, and if it wasn't as high as that of the pilots, he would be told so by the rest of the team. So, all the work the team does has to have a set standard to be achieved.

During the first year, the pilots work up to this standard, whereas third year pilots seemed to be 'guardians' of the standard.

> 'You are more critical and have more input in the third year than the other guys because you have seen it and been at the other end of the criticism. The reasons for the criticisms are to get the standard up to what we know we can do, but it is done light-heartedly. Our role in the third year is more involved with the training aspect and keeping the standards up.' Third Year Pilot

To be the best is a worthy standard and not arrogant. Some of the top teams I work with believe they are the best in their business and my role is to show them how to improve their team performance to achieve the best consistently. Imagine how you would feel being part of a team which is recognised as the best. It feels good – motivating. This link is very much tied up with link 9 in the chain – a reward and feeling of pride for success. But it is linked here with personal development because to work to a high standard will mean having to develop yourself.

To summarise, the key points here are:

- standards of performance should be known to all team members;

- each team member is responsible for maintaining these;

- personal standards should be incorporated into these.

7

Individual development to do the job better

Personal growth and fulfilment

The danger from some team members in organisations is that they believe they know everything, but of course no one does. The challenge of life, and teams, is to keep on growing. In developing each team member's potential, the whole will benefit. For example, after each sortie, the pilots look at where they can improve and strive to keep improving by learning from their mistakes. This enables the team to reach the required standard for the Commander in Chief to inform them that they are ready to put on their red suits. Without each individual continually developing, this standard would never be reached.

'You understand very quickly everyone's own limitations, and you can watch and see who has strengths in certain areas and are very aware of your most limiting factor. One of the guys might not be too happy in a certain area, and I am quite prepared to go and spend a day or two working on that. That's the way ahead.'
Team Leader

The essence here is to learn from everything you do – or even what is done to you. 'The art of life is not controlling what happens to us, but *using* what happens to us.' This means that we grow instead of exist. The benefits of this are for both the individual and the team. The link here with regular reviews is crucial. It is through feedback that individuals can grow – without it, they never know what is possible.

Goethe said: 'Treat a person as he or she is and they will remain as they are. Treat a man or woman as they can and should be and they will become as they can and should be.' What have you learned about yourself since starting to read this book?

The process of fulfilment comes when a person knows they are growing and doing well, and it is recognised. The goal is for self-actualisation which is at the top of Maslow's hierarchy of needs (see Figure 10). To achieve this you have to know what it is you want to become. The most important exercise I ever did was early on in my career. It wasn't easy, but it has become something I do on a regular basis. Answer these questions for yourself.

- If the world were perfect, what would you like to do and achieve above all else?

- If you can't have that, what else would you like to do and achieve?

- What areas do you need to develop and grow to fulfil these?

When establishing their personal goals, many of the Red Arrows recognised that to achieve them they would have to develop themselves, and grow to become a 'better team player' or 'deal with the public' and 'become a skilled pilot'. This link, like the others, cannot be done in isolation. The pilots' fulfilment came after months, even years, of practice and feedback. With each team member developing his or herself, the team grows and develops too. The team members set a standard of performance and each strives towards that.

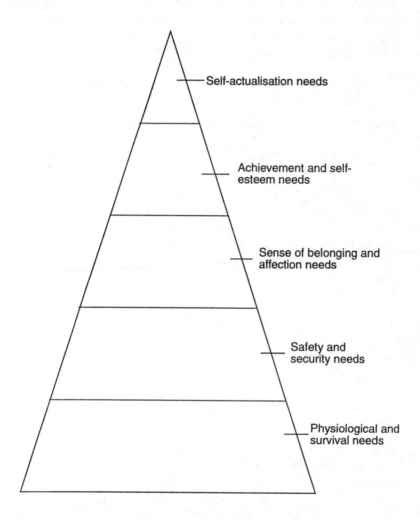

Figure 10 *Maslow's Hierarchy of Needs*

A Team Leader who ignores this link will prevent the team from achieving what is possible and giving the team members the experience of feeling fulfilled. Part of that personal development will include how team members relate to others outside the core team. Therefore, link 8 in the chain deals with this.

To summarise, the important points here are:

- by developing each team member's potential, the whole team will benefit;

- try to see every result as a learning step;

- fulfilment comes when you start towards where you want to go.

8

Positive inter-group relations with others outside the core team

Social needs and skills

No team can work totally in isolation. It has to relate and work with others. If it fails to do this, which is common, the team can fail and collapse. In addition, team members will need to belong with or communicate with others. This will differ between team members, so the Team Leader needs to be aware of this.

Answer this question honestly. What is more important to you: the task and to achieve; or to be accepted and liked by others in the organisation? We're all different – for some it will be the task; for others the social contact. The way to success and high performance is for team members to balance both.

Just as team members need to work effectively together, so too must different parts of the organisation work together in the corporate interest. If the pilots are ready to complete a summer season of giving over 100 displays, the 9 planes need to be in top condition to accomplish the task. Here the inter-relationships between the pilots and other teams is crucial.

The first inter-relating team is the travelling ground crew. These are 20 or more engineers who provide specialist support to sort out minor faults with the aircraft during the summer season on the road. They prepare the aircraft before each flight or display, checking to ensure that there are no cracks or damage to the frame or engine, refuelling, cleaning the aircraft, and replenishing the dye and diesel which makes the coloured smoke during the display. There can be as many as four of these pre-flight servicings a day. Some even get to fly in the Hawks, as each plane has its own engineer who flies with the same pilot and plane throughout the season to the destination. These nine engineers and the Engineering Officer are known as the 'circus', while the rest fly in the support Hercules or travel by road.

The second inter-relating team consists of the 40 rectification ground crew who are based at the Reds' base and carry out in-depth maintenance during the winter months while the pilots are developing the new display. During this period, spare aeroplanes are available. Each aircraft will take at least four weeks to be serviced. During breaks in the summer, when the planes are back at home, these engineers and technicians check the aircraft.

The third inter-group team is made up of the administration staff whose duties include organising the team's accommodation, booking the restricted airspace around each display, arranging diplomatic clearances for overseas displays, and organising the movement of the diesel and dyes for the coloured smoke. Each display venue has a mountain of paperwork which requires careful processing for the smooth running of the show and the safety of the public. During the winter months, the airbase has visitors and all the groundwork for the summer season is planned. These three teams work behind the scenes but are vital to the success of the Red Arrows. Each inter-relates with each other and others in the RAF, and it isn't all work.

'We have quite a busy social scene on the team and there are lots of opportunities to get together and get to know the guys. There's a bit of sport that goes on so we meet in that sort of environment as well. Mainly we work very closely together on a day-to-day basis and you very quickly get to know what the guys are like. There's a good healthy interaction that goes on.'
Engineer

But what about you in your organisation? Who relies on you to get it right? A good Team Leader recognises the need for networking, the need for information and resources, and the need for feedback about how the team is perceived. Therefore, inter-group relations are important to the success of the team.

Whom do you inter-relate with? How important is this relationship to the team? How can you improve this relationship so that both will benefit?

Where other teams in the organisation rely on you for service, they should be treated with as much respect as you give customers outside the organisation. Through having positive inter-group relations the team will achieve their goals and be perceived as a 'successful' team. This is motivating for everyone and becomes part of the 'reward' for hard work. The next link in the chain should maintain the effort and needs closer examination.

To summarise, the main points here are:

- you can't operate in isolation;

- inter-group relations will be easier for some than others – but all team members must work at it and this can include social activities;

- identify where both parties will benefit and concentrate on this.

9

A reward system for the whole team

Pride and commitment

For a reward system to be effective the reward should be linked to the performance of the whole team, rather than the individual performances. Everyone needs to feel valued and worth while. Therefore, a reward should say 'well done' to the team. It ensures commitment and should enable team members to feel proud of their results. An effective reward is rarely financial and is usually part of being something which is considered 'the best'.

The reward for the Reds is when the Commander in Chief tells them they are ready to put on their red suits. Up until now they have worn the usual green flying suits. The red suits signify that the required standard of performance has been met and they take great pride in wearing something which is recognised worldwide as being the best.

'It's been a hard work-up this winter, but it's been worth it.' Pilot on Red Suit Day

---

Linking rewards to the performance of the total team, rather than to individual performance, recognises the dynamic effect of group loyalty and teamwork as a powerful factor in individual motivation and development. When successful, the motivation of a team is increased as the members develop closer and stronger work relationships, and greater challenge and fulfilment in the work. In the case of the Red Arrows, the skills of the new pilots are built up gradually. As their skills, personal development and confidence grow, others are added in to the team. When they are comfortable with this, the manoeuvres become more complicated. The challenge becomes greater, but so too is the sense of the fulfilment on Red Suit Day when the pilots put their red suits on for the first time.

Teams in organisations need to find their own reward – but the most motivating is the fact that members belong to something which is exciting, challenging, recognised as the best and perceived as something others would like to be involved in.

To complete this link the team should:

- identify the key areas for success;

- set objectives, goals and performance targets;

- monitor progress and measure or evaluate performance;

- give feedback and review their success; and

- identify a reward which is valued by all team members.

Overseeing this, and the other links in the chain, is the Team Leader. How the Team Leader behaves and works through all the links is achieved through leadership based on respect rather than hierarchy, and is the final link in the chain.

The key points for this ninth link are:

- a reward should be linked to the team's performance, not individual performance;

- teams should take pride in their results;

- identify a reward which is valued by all team members.

10

Centred leadership which is appropriate for a high performing team

Consistency and balanced roles

It is no accident that this is the final link which joins the chain together to form a 'bracelet'. This link has to hold the chain together and make it great. To do this, the Team Leader has to lead as well as manage day-to-day matters. Leadership is the thrust here which will enable the team to achieve. I studied two Team Leaders of the Reds – each were very different with different leadership styles, but both were consistent and had the right balance of their roles as Team Leader. I asked John, the new leader, what he'd learned in his first year as Team Leader.

> 'The main thing I learned is that I can't do it all on my own. I'm no different from most people, I am just not that good. The one thing I learned very early on was I needed the experience that was around me . . . the three or four guys who've been around quite a while. And we would go through exactly what we were going to do that day, the way we were going to plan it. . . It kept me on

the straight and narrow, it kept them involved, and it meant that when I got up and briefed the sortie, it was going to go right because the more experienced heads had been round there. I did not lose any authority because of that. I was still the boss.' Team Leader

Management and leadership are different, using different skills and attitudes. Management concentrates on how to accomplish certain things; a leader asks, 'What are the things I want to accomplish?' Very often you can observe a team and Team Leader at the start of a project, and see them get totally engrossed in how they are going to do things. Instead, the first thing a Team Leader should ask is 'What do we want to achieve?' This links with objectives and goals (the next link when the chain is joined up), and while the team are working these out, the role of the team leader is to ensure that the 'what' has been answered.

To develop the right leadership the internal processes are balancing the roles of team leader and being consistent in your behaviour. As Team Leader you will no doubt have several roles to oversee. The Team Leader of the Reds has to balance being the officer for the squadron and getting the administration work complete, representing the squadron in other parts of the RAF and outside the organisation, as well as ensuring the team perform to the required standard for the summer season. By involving other team members and delegating properly, the Team Leader of the Reds was able to concentrate on the overlapping parts of those different roles. Therefore, the key to this is to identify your main roles and where they overlap. Then work on the important overlapping parts and involve others to oversee the rest.

What are your roles as Team Leader? Do you find that you are consumed by one or two of your roles at work and that the others do not receive the time and attention you'd like to give them? Do the roles work together to contribute to fulfilling your goals? Do you see yourself trying to balance and achieve them by running from one to another on a regular basis, and spending as much time as you can on each?

Instead, identify the roles you have as Team Leader and try to see them as overlapping. Each Team Leader's roles will differ, but design your own diagram to suit your roles. Now concentrate your time on the areas which overlap, instead of running between them and getting exhausted. This will make you delegate to team members who will then feel you are not tightly controlling everything to the extent that they feel they can't move. At the same time you will find you have more energy and will achieve more. This is how the Team Leaders of the Reds were able to do a highly demanding job.

In contrast I see time and again Team Leaders in organisations so busy trying to do everything, they don't have time to concentrate on those important overlapping parts. Decisions are slow and people are either frustrated or sit back and don't take ownership or responsibility for their own tasks. In this scenario, individual development is non-existent and the performance of the team is mediocre. By concentrating on the important overlapping parts, results are more effective and the Team Leader is able to achieve the 'what' by:

- getting to know the team as individuals; their values, attitudes, what motivates them, thus highlighting open and honest communication;

- ensuring that individuals know clearly what is expected of them, by discussing goals and changes which affect the individuals, rather than changing things without consultation;

- giving people a sense of belonging where there are no people who are 'in' and others who are 'out';

- giving focus and positive feedback about performance routinely, not just at appraisal time, to help motivate and develop team members;

- showing individuals that their contribution and role is recognised and valued by giving praise or thanks appropriately;

- looking for ways to give individuals opportunities for responsibility, autonomy, achievement and recognition through delegation;

- encouraging individuals to fulfil their self-development needs;

- ensuring that team members are capable of the tasks assigned to them, and have the proper resources and equipment.

The Team Leader has to be a model for the team. The past Team Leader of the Reds said that he had previously experienced two role models, one of which he tried to model himself on because he considered him to be a good Team Leader. If a leader is aiming to build a group where individuals:

- have high personal and team standards,

- work as a team and achieve their goals,

- confront issues as they arise, and are open and honest in their communications and relationships,

- use judgement and their initiative, and take responsibility for their actions,

then they need to model that behaviour themselves in their work and work relationships. This was highly visible in the new Team Leader for 1994. He had a difficult act to follow, but quickly showed his own style through following the above methods. His acceptance as Team Leader and credibility were quickly acknowledged. The following list shows how the Team Leader achieved this and how you can follow suit.

- Be true to your personal beliefs and be regarded as having integrity by others.

- Face facts and problems honestly.

- Be open, not manipulative in your dealings.

- Give trust and loyalty to the team, and support it strongly both inside and outside the group.

- Be accessible and receptive to others, and respect their needs.

- Use delegation to aid achievement and personal development, not only as a way of reducing your own work load.

- Be reliable in establishing clear goals and standards, and effective working practices.

Also, in doing this, the basis of any team is created – that is, trust between the leader and the team.

Trust doesn't happen overnight, it develops through consistency, predictability and reliability. This did not happen in a top team of a high-tech company because the Team Leader did not say what he meant, did not mean what he said, gave information which was unreliable, did not listen, was too self-interested, did not meet commitments, did not openly face up to issues which needed to be resolved, betrayed confidences, talked about others behind their backs and continually rushed around fire-fighting.

A high performing Team Leader behaves consistently and this enables the team to trust them. If a leader has favourites in the team or is seen to be harder on some, the trust will evaporate. Put consistent actions and behaviour together, and you are on the way to becoming an appropriate centred leader, reaching out to all the components. Think of an occasion where you had to deal with a difficult situation, but it went right. Now think of another difficult situation where things went terribly wrong. What were the differences in each situation? How can you be consistent in the future so that a difficult situation will work out?

It will be consistency and balancing your roles that will enable you to lead a high performing team. Consistency in resolving problems is improved if you realise the difference between leadership and management. Instead of seeing a problem as segmented – a broken piece to be mended – leadership sees it as part of a systematic whole. Management takes it to pieces, good leadership looks at what's around the problem, what's connected to it, what can be influenced to change it, as well as the problem itself.

However, there is something else to act on to finalise the process. In dealing with the team process, the Team Leader also has to take into account factors such as the degree of acceptance or inclusion of members in the team which is often indicated by the amount of verbal participation. It was interesting to watch the new Red Arrows team members become more and more confident in their verbal participation from first working with the team, to the point of putting on their red suits for the first time. In the autumn months they had been quiet and listened most of the time. By the time we were in Cyprus in May, they were giving as good as the other team members.

However, the degree of influence people have in the team may not be reflected in their participation. The members listened to weren't always the most vociferous. The way group decisions are arrived at can range from subgroups to the whole team participating. Any major decisions with the Reds were always taken by the team as a whole, with the Team Leader making the final decision if necessary.

The need for task and maintenance functions to be looked after was shared by the team in the Red Arrows, each relying on the others to do their job correctly. To create an open communications climate in the team the Team Leader should contribute by:

- being open and honest in their own communications, but focusing any suggestions for improvement on the job being done;

- sharing information, ideas, concerns and problems with team members;

- listening to and respecting the integrity of others in the team with different views;

- receiving 'bad' news about a situation, or differing views, or critical feedback about their own decisions and actions without reacting negatively or personally.

If, however, a Team Leader takes no action when told of impending problems, or becomes defensive or hostile to people in the face of disagreements, team members will react similarly themselves and in addition are likely to stop communicating information which produces hostile or negative reactions. A high performing Team Leader works on all the links in the synergy chain process and, by doing so, joins them together to form a strong chain to achieve the best results – a synergy chain.

We can summarise the key points here by saying:

- the role of the Team Leader is to concentrate on the 'what'; the team will decide the 'how';

- the Team Leader must be consistent and balance his or her roles to maximise results;

- the Team Leader has to ensure that each link in the synergy chain process is constantly strengthened.

PART III

6

Looking to the Future

"We need a fresh vision of business enterprise. In a society that has become predominantly urban and suburban we need a form of work organisation, and a work ethic, that offers men and women a certain scope, a certain dignity and freedom, and not just an existence."

George Godyer,
British International Paper Ltd.

"I believe increasingly that in the future the organisation will have to adapt to the needs of the individual, rather than expecting the individual to adapt to the needs of the organisation. This is not necessarily as anarchic as it sounds. Adaptation to the individual will release energies, creativity and imagination of a different order from that generated by the outfit which expects conformity to somebody else's wisdom. It does mean a radical change of thinking, and a much greater attempt to understand both the generality of expectation and the degrees of flexibility which individuals may require as a condition of their service."

Sir John Harvey-Jones, *Making it Happen*

At the beginning of this book I explained some of the changes affecting organisations today and their relevance to teamwork. To conclude I would like to show you how some organisations look today, how this is different, and why creating top flight teams is vital in organisations today and tomorrow.

ORGANISATION TYPES

During the 1970s and 1980s it became recognised that most organisations were based on those described by Charles Handy in *Understanding Organisations*. Here, Handy showed these organisation types by structure and culture (see Figure 11).

The first was the 'power' culture where a strong entrepreneur was at the centre, a top team around that person and the rest much further away. The power was at the centre and this proved problematic as the organisation grew. These organisations could be abrasive and tough, with low morale and high turnover at the middle layers, but were competitive and successful too. However, if the centre dies they can become obsolete. Examples of this range from the businesses run by Henry Ford and Robert Maxwell, to smaller family businesses.

The second organisation was the 'role' culture, often associated with bureaucratic types of organisations. Its strength lies in its functional departments, each working on their own, where people do their job and no more. Power is at the top which is distant from everyone else, including customers or the people they serve. Their weakness is their resistance to change, as it is based on rules and procedures which must be obeyed. Innovation is not valued. Many public sector organisations were run on these lines, as were the banks. Have they changed today?

The third type was the 'task' culture which looked like a net of project teams or task groups working to respond quickly to change. Its strength is its flexibility, but its weak-

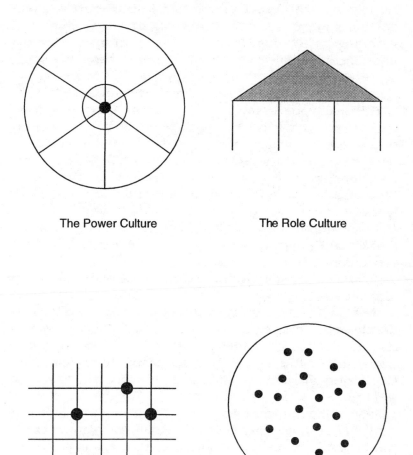

The Power Culture

The Role Culture

The Task Culture

The Person Culture

Figure 11
From *Understanding Organisations* by Charles Handy

ness is inability to develop large economies of scale. Often the product becomes the driving force and the best people are put on the most important projects. Expertise is the dominant power source and rewards are based on results. Examples include high-tech companies, but many organisations, including those who once were or still are in the public sector, are trying to adopt this way of working. Yet changing structures doesn't equate with changing cultures.

The final type was the 'person' culture where the individual is important. This type can be seen today in some firms of lawyers or management consultants. Again, power is often based on expertise. However, over time the organisation develops its own identity and starts to impose on the individuals. It can then become any of the previous three types.

Today, these organisations remain but are changing rapidly and new organisations are emerging which look very different (see Figure 12).

Whereas the old-style hierarchy emphasised looking up to bosses and doing as you were told, some have now put customers at the top. Pepsico turned its pyramid chart upside down and put the salespeople at the top to emphasise the focus on customers. Others, such as WL Gore, which makes the famous GoreTex fabric, have developed the task organisation into a 'lattice' structure with non-hierarchical relationships between jobs.

Semco, the pioneering and much written about Brazilian company, does not have a formal written organisation chart. But its leader, Semler, describes it as a small inner circle of counsellors (ex-directors), surrounded by a small circle of partners (leaders of the business units), surrounded by a huge circle representing everyone else with co-ordinators (ex-supervisors) as moving triangles. However, responsibility is throughout.

Finally, Eastman Chemical Company, a spin-off from Eastman Kodak, identify their model as a 'pizza' with the 'big-cheese' in the centre and managers/team members dotted around like pepperoni. The circles and spaces represent the flexible, cross-functional teamwork that has replaced hierarchies.

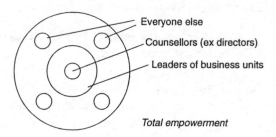

Everyone else

Counsellors (ex directors)

Leaders of business units

Total empowerment

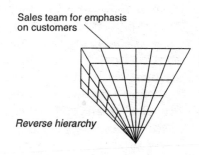

Sales team for emphasis
on customers

Reverse hierarchy

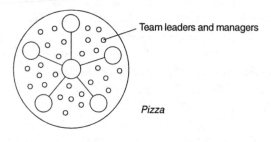

Team leaders and managers

Pizza

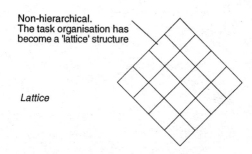

Non-hierarchical.
The task organisation has
become a 'lattice' structure

Lattice

Figure 12
*This is just a selection of a large assortment of organisations
today. The difference today is the growing variety.*

THE GROWING VARIETY

We have looked at four very different organisation structures and cultures – but this is only a sample of what is developing. The difference today is the growing variety. The structure of Virgin Airways puts customers at its centre and remains a first choice for many business transatlantic commuters, whereas others put product innovation or sales at their centre. What can be confidently said is that as organisations become flatter, teamwork will grow and become the norm, as will the need for new kinds of working relationships. Creating top flight teams, using the synergy chain process, is an example of such a new way for organisations where performance is required. This leads to developing a true team rather than a structure of teams who are groups of people who happen to work together.

Today, top flight teams are required at all levels in all organisations. We've heard a great deal about 'empowerment', but in most organisations there has been no transfer of power. There has been delayering, downsizing and restructuring, leaving low morale, overwork and a feeling that opportunities for career advancement are gone. This is because the old perception of organisations and careers, and the old cultures, still remain and the 'human' side of this organisational change has not been considered thoroughly.

Putting people together and calling them teams is not the solution either, while these old perceptions and cultures remain. This isn't just the fault of management either. I visit organisations where a small number of vocal employees moan about everything, but at the same time wallow in keeping up the 'them and us' scenario because they fear change and at least they know this 'devil'. Yet, having worked with some of these organisations, I know it is possible to change with the right strategy and actions.

A commitment to develop organisations for the future has to begin by the board becoming a top team, followed by everyone else. The organisation has to change to enable these teams to develop. Will Hutton wrote in *The*

State We're In that change must come in our political and economic organisations – I believe we have to add to that other organisations including businesses. He wrote: 'Britain in the 1990s has lost its sense of direction and its people are at odds with themselves. It needs to revitalise its economy, modernise its institutions, rewrite the contract between the members of its society and recover its self esteem.' This has to be extended to the organisations which employ us. They need to use the ideas and talents of all the workforce to compete. We have to change the perceptions of those managing and leading these organisations as well as the employees working there. Business leaders have to realise that tinkering with structures alone is not the answer. It also requires a change in power and leadership.

At present there is still a belief that management are responsible for the performance of their people. This propagates the belief that management should have the power and resources to achieve this. In this mindset, leadership is based on power being a limited resource and, if some is given away, the leader will have less. Therefore, people hang on to it. Changing structures alone will not change much. We have to believe that management's job is to empower people and make them responsible for their own performance. This for many is frightening, and resistance can come from both manager and employee.

James A Belasco and Ralph C Stayer explain the changes required in a recent paper entitled 'Why Empowerment Doesn't Empower: The Bankruptcy of Current Paradigms'. Here they argue: 'The leadership systems currently in use are designed to control relatively uneducated, mostly untrustworthy people in an environment of very slow change. In our free and democratic society, employees park their rights – along with their brains – at the door. Companies today are the last remaining feudal enclave.' However, the most feudal can change if the workforce are truly empowered and teams permeate throughout. This is the power of top flight teams.

TOWER COLLIERY

In 1984, the UK saw one of the most serious of coal strikes where everyone lost out. Today, there is a working mine in South Wales which has gone through a paradigm shift, and where teams throughout the workforce and management have enabled the mine to be a success and profitable. During the early 1990s British Coal decided that Tower Colliery would survive, along with one or two others on a medium to long-term basis. Other pits were closing, but Tower had some investment. However, British Coal then decided to close Tower as its potential was only 10 to 20 million tons, while others had the potential of well in excess of 20 million tons.

In April 1994, the pit closed for eight months, men were laid off and a skeleton staff of managers stayed to keep the infrastructure going. Production had ceased but British Coal would try and sell the colliery, even though there were no existing markets or contracts for the mine. A National Union of Mineworkers official, Tyrone O'Sullivan, along with others, asked themselves the question: Why can't we buy our own pit? A steering committee was formed to represent employees and keep them informed of developments. Soon all the men put in £2,000 of their redundancy money to start financing a buy-out.

There were other interested parties in the buy-out, but during October/November 1994 it was revealed that the Tower employees were the preferred bidders. At this point, the miners raised another £6,000 each from every employee who had put in £2,000 and worked on improving their business plan with help from the Trades Union Congress and Price Waterhouse. At this stage, a management team, including former managers of Tower Colliery, was formed to join the buy-out. Today, Tower Colliery is profitable with contracts worldwide. How was this brave achievement successful?

Andrew Walker, the safety engineer, told me that change started before the buy-out. Under British Coal there had been poor communications and a strong hierarchy which was affecting safety issues. To short-circuit these problems, Andrew put a team of strong individuals from all aspects of the workforce together to deal with safety. However, this teamwork led them to see that improved communication led to improved trust and productivity, and a working together mindset developed. When the buy-out happened the team mindset stayed. Therefore, the team infrastructure was there and the attitudes were right. Today the miners are the new co-owners with fewer management layers. Miners have worked in teams for a long time, but today at Tower they are more open and trust each other and their Team Leaders. They are 'top flight teams'.

Everyone has 8,000 shares and you can't sell your shares to someone else – thus preventing one person owning more than others. If you leave you sell your shares back to the company and they sell them to another miner who joins. These shares give voting rights for deciding on board members. Management vote for three board members and the employees vote for two. The board decide policy, for example to produce 450,000 tons a year; management and employees implement this and make the day-to-day decisions. Today management and workers work together, whereas previously, the style of management was to crack whips and the employees dragged their heels.

Ninety five per cent of the people working at Tower worked there under British Coal – the same men are doing the same job, but it is *very* different. Andrew Walker says it's because they 'own' the business – not just financially or even that they have more involvement – but because it is *their* business. They have pride and self-esteem in that ownership, as well as money invested.

One of the miners explained that 'Miners have always perceived the mines as owned by the people, but previously managers had their own canteen, were called Mr, had their own showers and even own loo paper. It's those little things that have changed. The old world, macho management has gone. Today we're all part of one team pulling together as equals. Whereas before there had been two languages, two perceptions, now managers listen to us and treat us as human beings. Today, managers go down the pit and talk to the men, whereas previously, they said what they wanted and cracked a whip. Today, management tap the ideas of people, so employees can influence, can get involved in the decisions and most importantly can use their brains.'

USING EMPLOYEES' KNOWLEDGE

Today organisations succeed because of the brains and knowledge of the workers – not manufacturing processes. Markets are now global, electronic highways enable instant communication and responses, and work involves the knowledge and information of the employees. This knowledge is not only in the heads of the leaders – it is throughout the organisation. We still tend to see knowledge as hard data and numbers, but we should include the skills and ideas of all workers. It is hard to share all this knowledge, but top flight teams in organisations capture innovation and commitment.

The aim today is for leaders to adopt this new way of working because if they don't, they will fail. These days it isn't enough to produce a plan and get people to implement it. Today, leaders have to produce a plan that will be owned and understood by those who have to execute it. This is built on sharing power and responsibility, and on a culture of trust. Therefore power, leadership and management have changed as well as structures and cultures. Today, leaders lead through trust and employees manage. This is how the Red Arrows produce world-class performance – and have fun and satisfaction doing it. It is our challenge, but 'Challenges make you discover things about yourself that you really never knew. They're what make the instrument stretch – what make you go beyond the norm' (Cicely Tyson).

The challenge for the Red Arrows is to come to the team from an organisation which is changing, becoming flatter, and develop the synergy chain process through the winter months to become a top flight team by summer. The challenge for Tower Colliery is to be profitable and sustain a workforce for many years.

This is what is possible when teams are allowed to flourish. It can even go beyond a company and be the ethos of a country. In South Africa there is a concept its people are taking to heart. It's called the Spirit of Ubuntu which means 'I am, because you are'. It also means the team is greater than the individual and this we saw demonstrated at the final of the Rugby World Cup in 1995. ITV commentator Alan Hignell summed it up when he said: 'This rainbow nation, all behind their team.' This was reinforced by South Africa's rugby team captain Francois Pienaar who said: 'One team: one country.' But living that Spirit of Ubuntu was South Africa's President Nelson Mandela, wearing a player's shirt and cap in the 'old' colours of South Africa.

The country had become one team and, with it, self-esteem had returned. It had two Team Leaders in Mandela and Pienaar, whose consistency won the belief and trust of their nation. On this emotional day of hard physical endeavour and success, both black and bokke were united behind these two men.

It is ironic that in 1995 the Red Arrows were on tour in South Africa where their performances were watched by many of the people who watched the rugby. There is so much to learn here for organisations and it begins with Ubuntu – belief in the team. There is a belief at the heart of the Reds in what they do. It is a belief other organisations must adopt, not only because it will enable the talents and brains of the workforce to be used, but it will also enable organisations to perform at their greatest level. This is the challenge for organisations and the people in them.

DEVELOPING HIGH PERFORMING TEAMS IN ORGANISATIONS

To develop high performing teams in organisations means to make a conscious commitment as well as taking actions. This is because one action can counteract another. A well-known manufacturing company, with its products in most homes, has spent time and money training people to be teams and set up cell manufacturing structures. However, a new managing director, whose personal actions in the first few weeks demonstrated self-interest rather than team interest, has resulted in people remaining sceptical and mistrusting what they were told. Therefore, working with the board is the first step to ensure *real* change.

This begins with diagnostic work to establish which links are working and which are not. From this, a programme is constructed which is right for that particular team. Every link is developed, but some need more work than others. It also means that issues such as self-esteem, being open, being consistent and so on are taken on board by the top team, and they realise how important these areas are for others. Therefore, the synergy chain process can influence change in the culture, attitude and behaviour of the organisation. The team have to believe it, feel it and act it out consistently.

Working with boards of directors is a challenge, but it is where this work has had greatest impact. The stumbling block is always whether the Team Leader wants the board to be a team or believes it is perfect and doesn't need to change. In both situations I hear senior managers below tearing their hair out with frustration but feeling powerless.

Once this work is complete, other teams follow the process, each having their own emphasis, relative to their needs. Follow-up visits ensure that the process is working and if there is a problem, follow-up work is carried out. This is no 'quick fix' solution. It can be a long process, particularly for some organisations. For others, one or two programmes are enough and the changes permeate the organisation. Working with the top team enables the changes necessary for top flight teams to flourish and performance to enhance. It means that what is said is believed and taken on board or 'owned' by every employee from director down, because behaviour by Team Leaders is consistent. It enables the values of people to become part of that organisation and teams have the power to act.

For those sceptics who ask 'Isn't this just another fad?' my reply is definitely not. Teams have been around a long time – but identifying roles and constructing building blocks does not go far enough to bring the changes required for top flight teams. Bernard Sullivan, General Manager of Rover Learning Business, was for many years the Training Manager of LandRover where he saw a culture change and teams develop. He argues that as well as a common purpose being important, that common purpose or goal must be tied to personal needs and goals.

Alistair Wright, who was Human Resource Director of Digital Equipment, says: 'Feedback is core to teamwork, which is about people interacting. Team members have to be able to give and receive feedback positively and constructively. In order to achieve this, I believe individuals need to develop their own self-esteem and self-understanding.' He also believes a team should share values.

It's not a case of which one is right – they both are. Everything these two experts on human development say is part of the synergy chain process. But there also needs to be agreement on, for example, standards of performance, and a reward system which gives ownership and pride. It is clear that each link is important and each must work together. This is how to develop teams in organisations. It's not a fad – but a dynamic process which some have taken on board and they are thriving as a result.

Finally, this is not a solution to resolve all difficulties. Restructuring organisations has created its own problems. Poor communications are still affecting the performance of many organisations. Even positive initiatives such as

Investors in People have opened a Pandora's box for some organisations which fail to reach the required standard because the initiative isn't owned by management or employees, where it's become yet another task for pressurised people to cope with, often because the only force is that the director wants the plaque on the wall. Creating top flight teams will move organisations forward to becoming the best without a bureaucratic implementation process.

Learning how the Red Arrows develop their team to world-class performance will enable organisations to create top flight teams to deal with a fast changing world. This work will equip people to respond to a world market and compete, knowing the sky's the limit for them too. As well as soaring in the sky and thrilling thousands with their displays, the Red Arrows are now reaching organisations and helping them too.

Rosabeth Moss Kanter, in her book *When Giants Learn to Dance*, summarises what for me is the most important message to people in organisations today when going through any transition: 'to perceive that their fate is shared and they can help one another.' This is the Spirit of Ubuntu and rooted in the RAF Red Arrows and the commitment of the synergy chain process in creating top flight teams in organisations today.

POSTSCRIPT

7

Personal Reflections

> "A woman's life can really be a succession of lives, each revolving around some emotionally compelling situation or challenge, and each marked off by some intense experience."
>
> *Wallis Simpson, Duchess of Windsor*

When I heard the team manager of the RAF Red Arrows talking about his team I recognised something that looked as though it had potential to help organisations. I stepped into that world and discovered more than a theory – it was a belief and philosophy centred on being the best. For the last decade or more, I have seen business practices being adopted across other organisations that have been inhuman, yet accepted as the norm. I have seen an army of 'consultants' who believe that because they have 20 plus years' experience of business, they can advise others, and have gone in after them to pick up the pieces. I have seen managing directors tinker with structures and processes, believing this will enable them to compete better, but afraid of 'real' change and loss of control. I have seen managing directors sign up to initiatives such as Opportunity 2000, but tell their managers that on no account are they to do anything to develop women as it will upset the men. This is not how to be the best.

In this other world, however, I saw a team which had

developed a way of being the best year after year. The work was challenging and the passion for flying soared. This world was very 'male', but it was good fun for women too. There was chauvinism, particularly at the higher levels, but it was changing slowly. Like other organisations this tended to be a generation issue, as the pilots themselves felt the same opportunities should be there for women. The Team Leader said: 'If my daughters decide on a career in the RAF, I want them to have the same opportunities I've had.'

I felt part of that team, especially during the first year. I was made so welcome and had to develop my bantering skills to deal with the humour. On my first trip to Cyprus I had to cope with the two-hour time difference and was challenged on my second morning to meet the guys for breakfast at 6.00 a.m., which for me was still 4.00 a.m. I made it, but felt and looked like a zombie! I wasn't going to fail to rise to the challenge. On the airstrip in Cyprus where the team practised daily, there were only men's toilets. When one of the female officers or myself needed to use them, someone had to first check there was no one inside, then wait outside to stop anyone coming in while we were in there. It was something you just accepted and had to see the funny side of.

Every afternoon at 4.00 p.m. you could go to the Mess for tea and toast with jam. This made it feel like home for me although keeping the conversation to a whisper was sometimes difficult, but some outsiders said it smacked of old imperialism.

During the week the team tended not to drink alcohol and go to bed early, but this was made up for at weekends when everyone could relax. During the first year we had an evening with the Air Vice-Marshal at a restaurant and this was one of my happiest memories. After eating, we played after-dinner games which everyone had to join in with and I could see that this was all part of developing the team as much as the flying. It was great fun with a strong sense of 'belonging'.

Yet within this world I also saw people promoted not

because of their ability, but because they were good at presenting themselves and their achievements, just as in any other organisation. I felt some irritation at seeing the quiet, hard-working pilots not getting the promotion. It wasn't perfect and I wouldn't expect it to be. But the people were different. The cynicism, the bitterness and anger I have seen in organisations weren't there. These people were confident, and had purpose and pride in their work. I felt so happy to be part of that world for a short while. Isn't that what work should feel like every day?

I have to admit to getting too close to the team during the first year and felt sad that when the third year pilots left there had been no goodbye. I often wonder what those pilots are doing now and realise that I was just another one of the huge number of people they come into contact with while they are Red Arrows. But for me it was so much more. To discover what it was they did to be the best I had to get close to them and know how they felt, what they believed in and how they saw themselves. I ended up feeling terribly protective about them – on one occasion they had to fly very close to prohibited airspace and I didn't relax until they returned.

The best memory which will always stay with me happened on my first day on one of the beaches on the base. I had gone off on my own to think through clearly my objectives for that week and to work on the format of some of the research. I was totally alone on the beach as everyone works until lunchtime because they start very early. The heat in the afternoons makes it very difficult to work when you're not used to it.

I had been on the beach for about 15 minutes when the team suddenly flew over. They were using the sea as a crowd line and for the next 20 minutes I had my own personal display right in front of me. It was striking to see the red planes against blue sky and sparkling sea. I don't think they knew I was there, but it is a unique memory I will always have. It is one I will never forget.

My biggest regret and sadness was that I never experienced flying in one of the jets. Even today, when I see the team fly my feelings are a mixture of the excitement that has never vanished, and a sadness that I will never know the feeling of flight. Having flown other planes, I can only imagine what it is like. It is a deep sadness I will always have and nothing will change that. The reason is a weight restriction which came into being following a crash and badly burned pilot from a Harrier who was caught in a fireball and, although there is no conclusive evidence, there are some who believe that weight in the ejector seat was a contributory factor. It is also unfortunate that the weight limit will tend to affect women rather than men.

However, the sadness is compensated for because I was to discover a theory that could change other people's working lives if they were given the chance. I had found a way of developing people to be the best, to be part of something that could give them fulfilment and pride. The synergy chain process is more than a theory – it is a perception, a philosophy which when put into practice, releases the potential of people and organisations. For that I will always be grateful.

Today, the programme developed from this theory is helping boards of directors to be more effective. It is also helping managers and employees. So, although I'll never fly in a fast jet, I'm getting a buzz working with top teams. The video has become part of a training package with The Industrial Society. This includes a workbook for trainers, video, handouts and OHPs. There are also training courses for people who want to run the programme. The package enables all employees to experience the Red Arrows' approach to high performing teams but, in addition, the proceeds from the training package are going to the Red Arrows Trust Fund which donates money to a variety of needs. Therefore, the project has a worthwhile outcome, reaching more than companies.

Flying and aeroplanes will always be part of my life. But my work as a management consultant has been given a clearer direction and future. Yet this work does not encompass everything. I still work developing organisations that need to change and developing women to become leaders. But this project was fun and challenging, and when I go back to see clients I see that changes have become part of the reality of those organisations.

In return we must ensure that defence cuts do not take this important team away. For not only are they a PR vehicle for the RAF for recruitment, and an example of excellence in the world of the Armed Forces, but the team is now helping other organisations develop people to become top flight teams all over the world.

Bibliography

Adair, John (1987) *Effective Team Building*, Pan Books, London

Garratt, Robert (1990) *Creating a Learning Organisation*, Institute of Directors, London

Handy, Charles (1985) *Understanding Organisations*, Penguin, Harmondsworth

Handy, Charles (1989) *Age of Unreason*, Business Books, London

Harvey Jones, John (1988) *Making it Happen*, Collins Glasgow

Hutton, Will (1995) *The State We're In*, Random House, London

Johnson, Mike (1995) *Managing in the Next Millennium*, Butterworth Heinemann

Kanter, Rosabeth Moss (1984) *The Change Masters*, Allen & Unwin, London

Kanter, Rosabeth Moss (1990) *When Giants Learn to Dance*, Allen & Unwin, London

Manchester Open Learning (1992) *Achieving Goals Through Teamwork*, Kogan Page, London

Morgan, Gareth (1989) *Creative Organization Theory*, Sage Publications, London

Peters, Tom (1989) *Thriving on Chaos*, Pan Books, London

Semler, Ricardo (1993) *Maverick*, Century

Woodcock, Mike (1979) *Team Development Manual*, Gower, Aldershot

Index